THE LITERARY LION.

THE

LORGNETTE:

OR,

STUDIES OF THE TOWN.

BY

An Opera Goer.

QUID LIBET, CUI LIBET, DE QUO LIBET.

SECOND EDITION,

SET OFF WITH MR. DARLEY'S DESIGNS.

New York.

Printed for STRINGER AND TOWNSEND,

And for sale at 222 Broadway, and all respectable Book-shops.

EDWARD O. JENKINS, PRINTER AND STER.,
114 Nassau street, New York

TO MY

READERS

HIS Preface is written for the Public; and by virtue of it, and of the bookbinder's work in clapping together these letters, first written to a friend in the country, I make over the business of finding fault with them, or praising them, to the wise and talkative world.

I have got very little to say here, which may not be found said in some shape or other, in the book itself; nor have I any flattery in hand for obstinate readers, to make them either lenient, or kindly disposed. Yet I have a tolerably good opinion of the public, and think it, as the times go, wise, considerate, and charitable; and so thinking, I have not felt it worth my while to hatch out any brood of lies, as is the custom with most new authors, about my modesty, and diffidence, and Heaven knows what.

As for Apology, I have got none to make;—except to say that the matter was not made up out of spitefulness or malice toward any man or woman; on the contrary, my feelings are tender toward the men in general,—and women specially. If anybody thinks otherwise, and feels worked up to such a pass, that he means to retort, I would particularly caution him, as I would the Theologic disputants, against striking, before he knows what he is going to hit.

I cannot let the opportunity slip, without giving my thanks for the praises which have often greeted my ears; and to which, occasionally, a regard for my incognito, (to say nothing of truth) has compelled me to yield a reluctant assent. At other times, however, I have listened to abuse, especially from authors, which has made me bite my lip, and heartily wish myself in other company.

Not a few of the Journals have damned me with a little faint praise, and expressed candid regrets that so much 'refinement' belonged to my papers. I would not for a moment impugn the judgment of these gentlemen, and only regret my inability to satisfy their taste.

There is an old story of a school-boy, who sneered at a whip of nettles as a flimsy affair; but who was observed to rub the afflicted part, for a long time afterward. There may be times when a cowhide is the proper medium of admonition; but it always needs a braggart bully for the handling. God forbid that I, a stranger, and appearing as an actor on the

Literary stage only by courtesy, should interfere with the professional repute of such performers.

Finally, (for this Preface is getting longer than I meant it should,) I give up these twelve letters into the hands of my readers, with the greatest honesty imaginable ; and if they cannot think well of me, after they have got through them, I hope, at least, that they will not condemn too harshly, a work, which my love for them has prompted.

JOHN TIMON.

Dated from my Attic,
July the 10th, MDCCCL.

CONTENTS.

NUMBER ONE.

NUMBER TWO.

NUMBER THREE.

NUMBER FOUR.

NUMBER FIVE.

NUMBER SIX.

NUMBER SEVEN.

NUMBER EIGHT.

NUMBER NINE.

NUMBER TEN.

NUMBER ELEVEN.

NUMBER TWELVE.

THE LORGNETTE.

JAN. 20. NEW-YORK. NO. I.

Non hodie si
Exclusus fuero, desistam; tempora quæram;
Occurram in triviis; deducam.—Hor. 1 Sat. ix. 58.

You know, my dear Fritz, that I am not unused to the handling of a glass; and that I have amused myself for a considerable number of years in looking about the world, as carelessly and freely as I chose. Now, it has occurred to me, in the opening of this new half-century, (may you live to the end of it!) that in common justice, I ought to make such return as lies in my power, by attempting to amuse some little portion of that world, which has so long and gratuitously amused me.

You stare hugely, to find your old friend become a man of type, and making his New-Year's greetings in veritable print. But book-making, let me tell you, is now-a-days but a very small affair; since every blue-stocking thinks it worth her while to spin out rhymes for the lady journals; and the old class of wholesome authors in shabby coats, and dirty linen, is almost supplanted by a great tribe of coxcomb writers, in opera gloves, and in velvet trimmings.

I am aware that I am challenging, in this way, a degree of attention from the very enlightened public of the city, which possibly I may never get; and that I wantonly assume a task, which the world, in its wisdom, may decide to be wholly beyond my powers. But I console myself with the reflection, that in this affair of book-making, I have got no reputation to lose; and indeed, were it otherwise, I should be much disposed to question whether, in this day of mushroom growth, it would not be more creditable to lose reputation, than to gain it.

To fame, or to what passes for it now—to newspaper-mention, I am fortunately wholly unknown: Since the days of the old College catalogue,—with the exception, indeed, of some half dozen passenger rolls of Foreign Packets,—I do not remember ever to have seen my name in print; nor shall I flatter my vanity by heralding it now.

I shall lose thus, it is true, the sympathies of friends and acquaintances; for I shall maintain an incognito as strictly in the circles where I am cordially received, as in the public talk. My papers, then, will have no support of friends, and no hireling praise: on the other hand, I shall have no enemies who can throw an old and cherished bitterness into their condemnation. And this last, I reckon no small point; since the popular *littérateurs* of the city, as I am told, are forever quarreling, and barking at each other, like so many apes of Siam. Now, as the critical attachés to this amiable fraternity of town writers will have, in my case, no reputation to pull down, and no old grudge to satisfy, I have a hope of passing scot-free,—without so much as a single vagabond pen being wet to dampen my fire. But let me warn them, that if they choose to bark, they may bark till their lungs are sore, and they will draw out no newspaper card in reply, nor shall I suborn any of their fraternity to bolster me up.

It would be very idle to pretend, my dear Fritz, that in printing my letters, I had not some hope of doing the public a trifling service. There are errors which need only to be mentioned, to be frowned upon; and there are virtues, which an approving word, even of a stranger, will encourage.

Both of these objects belong to my plan; yet my strictures shall not be personal, or invidious. It will be easy, surely, to carry with me the sympathies of all sensible people, in a little harmless ridicule of the foibles of the day, without citing personal instance; and it will be vastly easier, in such Babylon as ours, to designate a virtue, without naming its possessor!

Still, you know me too well, to believe that I shall be frightened out of free, or even caustic remark, by any critique of the papers, or by any dignified frown of the literary coteries of the city.

My publisher, indeed, has assured me, that without favorable mention from such and such newspapers, my work would all be idle, and my toil all be damned in advance. One of the journals, he told me, if carefully treated with, would make the merits of my plan known to the whole fashionable world;—nay, that a breath of praise from that quarter, would make my letters, fashionable letters. He cited two or three books, which by a single half-column of commendation, had been secured the run of the town; and he assured me that not a few boarding-school misses were crazily in love with the authors bepraised by the journal in question; and moreover, that its editor had secured eligible husbands to some half dozen despairing literary spinsters, who had been honored with assiduous, and determined complimentary notices, at his hands.

Another journal, I was told, must be conciliated, or it would become rank assailant, both of my design and of its execution; though, by my publisher's own confession, it seemed quite questionable, if its assaults would not work me more favor, even than the prettiest of its compliments. Another, whose literary budget was most astutely managed by a keen admirer of the late Mr. Charles Fourier, would carry news of me to all the hotel tables of the town; and a flattering notice, if it could be secured, would make my papers particularly palatable to all who make a joke of society. A fourth, read at all tea-drinkings, and very safe for Sunday perusal, or for nervous invalids, would give me the stamp of propriety among good old ladies, and all *respectable* people: And yet another, by bare mention—if only the types did not get askew,—would make me matter of gossip with all such gadding, companionable housewives, as are forever on the look-out for terrible casualties, personal movements, and arrivals at the hotels.

My publisher farther suggested a connection with some one of those literary coteries, which he tells me belong to the reading population of the town, and which would trumpet my design in a quiet way, at social gatherings—make my papers a standard tea-topic, and flatter even my shortcomings.

Some of these coteries, he told me, had stated meetings, at which all new literary matters were discussed over coffee and ices; and that it needed only a rehearsal from the lips of some blooming *littèrateure* in bodice, and an approving word or two from some of the committee managers, to give to the work of a new writer the dignity of reputation.

To the suggestion in regard to the newspapers, which touched my publisher in a tender point—his purse—I replied, by enclosing him a cheque, which would secure him against all possible loss.

Of the coteries, I told him, I was wholly unknown; and as it would come into my plan to speak very freely of all such cliques as assume the privilege of giving to the town its literary opinions, I begged to be excused from making any overtures. Nor will I conceal the fact, that this decision of mine was sustained by the conviction that all such overtures, coming from one in my humble condition in the literary world, would be treated with rank disdain.

As for topic, it will vary with the week, and with

my humor. Somotimes I shall fill my papers with portraits, or such social usages as prevail, and as seem to me deserving of remark; and shall endeavor to give you an idea of our town life, by calling up to your eye appearances of street and playhouse. At other times, I shall hope to light your features into a smile, by sketching, in my careless way, the lounges and loges of the Opera, and perhaps an interior of City Salon—with this special and firm proviso, however—that in no instance the hospitality which may be accorded to me as a stranger, will be abused. You will understand, then, that when I speak of the receptions of such as Mistress Dolly Dragall—not that I have the honor of any such acquaintance, and am abusing a tender confidence,—but that I make her a type (if she really exist) of some particular usage, and hope honestly to do her honor, by extending the publicity of her charms, and to flatter her vanity by descanting on the suavity of her address.

Town coats, and costumes, and mantillas, will not be out of the range of my LORGNETTE, and any innocent little extravagances of hat, or pelisse, or shoe-tie, will be touched for your amusement, as daintily as the prettiest flower wreaths in the hands of Miss Lawson's girls.

I shall depict for you, from time to time, samples

of the different social stages and fashionable gradations which meet my eye; and shall try to satisfy your country curiosity, by testing their groundwork. You must not be surprised, indeed, my dear Fritz, if within the range of my glass, should come up some old country acquaintances, whom we remember years ago in pretty rustic *deshabille*, and with strong nasal twang,—now riding in carriages, emblazoned with such heraldry as does honor to the ingenuity of Collis and Lawrence!* Delicate work, you will say; but I know no reason in the world why fashionable pretensions, however noisy in their claims, or however successful in their empiricism, should be too high or too sacred for the curious and earnest gaze of a simple-minded looker-on, even though he avail himself of the slightly magnifying powers of a LORGNETTE.

As for literary opinions, and men, and books, they will drop into my papers at intervals; not so much as topic for learned and critical remark, as by way of weather-cocks to show how the current of town opinions is drifting. Book-making has become so much a matter of trade, mere accommodation of supply to demand, that it seems to me

* Eminent carriage manufacturers in New-York; who, if they are duly grateful for this allusion, will send one of their new Britskas to the editor of the LORGNETTE.

far more reasonable, on all principles of public economy, to rail at the readers of bad books rather than their writers.

Religious and moral habitudes—their tendencies and exhibitions—will without doubt, occasionally sweep over the field of vision, and if they do not pass so quickly as to render the effort vain, they shall be reduced to some sort of classification. Indeed, I shall make very free to speak of the innumerable bickerings and schisms, which, as I hear, belong to church life in town; nor between doubtful Bishops, and pungent Lady Alice in breeches, will the topic be without its sources of amusement. And if a little good-natured raillery may have the effect of rendering ridiculous such absurdities as belong to town practices of worship, I shall feel as if engaged in an Apostolic labor; and as if, without the laying on of hands, I were as good a servant of the Mother Church, as the leanest of the Bishops, or the fattest of the Vestry-men. Nor shall the Barnburners, wire-pullers, office-seekers, journalists, and other political *quidnuncs* be passed by unceremoniously. I promise you, they shall have their sittings. I might even adopt for motto, if it had not been adopted *ad nauseam*, that line of Terence:—

Nihil humani a me alienum puto.

And I could translate it with more freedom than would have been tolerated on the university benches,—nothing touches humanity, but touches me.

In short, my dear Fritz, this LORGNETTE of mine will range very much as my whim directs. In morals, it will aim to be correct; in religion, to be respectful; in literature, modest; in the arts, attentive; in fashion, observing; in society, free; in narrative, to be honest; in advice, to be sound; in satire, to be hearty; and in general character, whatever may be the critical opinions of the small littérateurs, or the hints of fashionable patrons, to be only—itself.

The LORGNETTE will puff no books or tarts. If any venders of such wares send them to the publisher, it must be at their own risk. If the tarts are good, they will be eaten; if the books are good, they will be kept. Of the two, I may frankly say, the tarts would be preferred.

LODGINGS IN TOWN.

Sunt bona, sunt quædam mediocria, sunt mala plura.—MARTIAL.

You shall now see what matter I have made of it, in searching out my winter's lodgings. In Europe, you know, it is of but little account where a stranger bachelor may live in a city. He is comparatively so little known or inquired for, *chez lui*, that he may inhabit garret or palace, as he fancies best. You will remember too, without doubt, our pretentious acquaintance of London, who, with a dusky chamber in Fleet street, received all his friends at a fashionable house of the new Palace Yard. His letters and cards being all addressed to the Hotel, and a small periodical fee to the head-waiter, secured not only their acceptance at his hands, but the post services of a little boy who ran, on the occasion of a call upon our acquaintance, from the hotel into Fleet street.

In Paris, even this sham appearance is unnecessary. Both you and myself have thought it no discredit to leave our address at the hotel of Madame C——, of the Place Vendome, dating from the eastern end of the dirty Rue Jacob. And you will recall with a smile, after so long a lapse of time, our raillery of a certain transatlantic friend, who thought it necessary to take brilliant apartments in the Rue de Hauteville, and to order his dinners from the Café de Paris, and who was so astonished to find his salon *accueil* so wofully disproportionate to the tale of his weekly expenses!

In New-York, as I am told, the case is very different; and a man is not a little estimated by the street he lives in, or the house from which he hails. An officious, but good-natured friend, who was possibly not aware that I possessed some previous acquaintance with the purlieus of the city, hinted to me that if I wished to take rank among what he called genteel people, I must take lodgings far up town. And another suggested, when I spoke of remaining at what seemed to me a very fair sort of hotel, that it would never do ; that the hotel was not at all the thing, and that a miserable attic in a fashionable up-town house, which he took the liberty of recommending, would be much more to my credit and standing. He even hinted, that if I persisted in remaining in such quarters, for their size and comforts, I should take frequent evening walks in the direction he had named, and so make a mock of living, where fashionable men made their head-quarters. He further told me, by way of inducement, of one or two individuals, who with a bare pittance to keep soul and body together, had nevertheless, by dint of scrupulous economy and nice exactitude in such matters, succeeded in passing a couple of seasons for men of wealth and ton, and had eventually carried off splendid fortunes in the doweries of retired mercers' daughters.

Now, as you know, my dear fellow, that I am not wintering in town to make a name, either with fashionable people, or fashion hunters, and that my age would exculpate me from all intentions upon retired mercers' daughters, I paid very little regard to any such suggestions.

I have lived long enough to consult the ease and comforts of life far more than appearances; and as I wished a quiet neighborhood, and one which should not be far removed from what would, in all probability, be my usual haunts, to wit, the Exchange, the Society Library, and the Club in which I have become enrolled, I determined to set at naught all opinions of place, and to take such lodgings as suited my fancy.

Among the advertisements which met my eye in the papers, not a few contained provisos to the intent, that references would be expected; I therefore supplied myself with a few of the cards of the mercantile houses to which I had been accredited, and which, at least, could substantiate my ability to pay for a year's lodging.

It was a wet, gloomy day on which I made my first trial, and I had put on an old pea-jacket which had seen much ocean service, and a very shabby hat. The landlady I first addressed—a stout buxom old lady in black and crimson calico, looked rather suspiciously at my coat, but prayed me to be seated,—remarked upon the weather, and from the weather ran on with a very glib tongue to the gaieties of the town. She begged to know if I had the acquaintance of Messrs. So and So, who had some time been lodgers in her house; hinted that perhaps I might know another gentleman who was in excellent society, a man of large fortune, and who visited Messrs. So and So; but finding me incorrigible on these points, and only anxious to secure a quiet, comfortable room, she restrained somewhat the glibness of her speech. Her rooms proved not at all to my taste.

Having bade her good morning, which she met with a very condescending sweep of her black and crimson calico, I found myself next in a dingy parlor, hung with faded damask curtains. A slattern girl, in very showy merino, who was thrumming at a piano sadly out of tune, met my entrance with a very low and supercilious bow, and continued her employment, which, so far as I could judge, was a succession of efforts to catch some of the worst, though most striking passages of *Don Pasquale.*

The landlady presently came in, trimmed off with a tremendous flounce, and curtseying and bowing together, in a way that might have taken a man of livelier temperament off his legs. I presented one of the cards of the commercial house, and begged to know if, under such recommendation, she would allow me the favor of looking at her rooms.

She assured me that she would be most happy; at the same time eyeing my coat and hat with that look of thorough curiosity, which I find belongs to lodging-house keepers in all parts of the world.

She informed me that the neighborhood was highly respectable, and that her lodgers were, many of them, connected with some of the first families of the town; and thereupon she commenced enumerating to me a galaxy of names, which she did with an air that she seemed to think would utterly confound and embarrass a man in such damaged pea-jacket as I happened to be wearing. I maintained, however, sufficient composure to bow very graciously at the announcement of each name, and to tell her plainly at the end, that I knew nothing of them.

She was evidently thwarted, but determined to try me next by her scale of prices. She ushered me into a dim, shabbily furnished upper parlor, which she assured me was a charming apartment, and had been occupied by a gentleman of high distinction in the town circles. She directed my especial attention to the fine heavy old furniture, which, to be sure, was heavy and old enough; but not finding me to join in her ecstasies, she asked if I had been long in the city?

On hearing that I had but recently returned from

a long residence in the country, she launched out into praises of town life:—had no doubt that I would find it delightful; and, glancing at the card, thought it would be easy to secure an introduction —indeed, she said she had frequent *sawraze* at her own house, at which a Mrs. Somebody was a frequent attendant; and she would, if I took her rooms, interest herself as much as possible in my behalf. She hoped I loved music; her daughter Fanny, she said, was "a *ammature*,"—possibly I might have remarked her execution in the parlor.

The truth was, Fanny's execution was even now painfully distinct, and utterly dissipated any thought I might have entertained of engaging rooms in so close proximity with the parlor instrument.

My next negotiation was with a little, thin, weazen-faced French lady, of a certain age, who was most earnest, notwithstanding my pea-jacket, with the praise of her *fort jolies* chambers. She smiled at my card of reference; plumed herself on being able to detect at a glance a lodger "*comme il faut*;"—complimented my French, and showed me such dirty apartments that I was fain to pay her back in her own coin, and ended with regretting that her charming rooms should be all so high, or so low, as to prevent my becoming a lodger with so gracious and interesting a young lady. We parted, of course, capital friends.

My next adventure was with a very prim and demure-faced little lady in black, occupying a small house, which she told me had been the property of her poor husband, who was now dead (and she sighed), and who had been well known on 'Change, where, if I chose, I could make inquiries which would satisfy me as to respectability. She showed me a quiet, neat-looking room, upon the second floor, looking out upon a small court, garnished with low roofs and brick walls, and a single sickly-looking espalier peach-tree. The furniture was simple, but substantial; a pleasant, "tasteful" gentleman, with his wife, she told me, occupied the front-room,—a very respectable old man was above, and her nieces, from the country, occupied the remaining attic.

I thought it would be a quiet place for my work, where I should be out of the reach and knowledge of prying eyes; and where, my dear Fritz, I could quietly entertain you, on your visits to the city;—so I closed with her terms, and am now writing from a little white table which stands before the grate.

The "tasteful" gentleman proves to be a dashing buck, who wears very broad plaid to his pantaloons; he has over-reached himself in marriage, and is now paying the forfeit in these quiet chambers, and only gratifying the old exuberance of his nature by an occasional Sunday dash, in buggy and pair, upon the Third Avenue. His wife, of whom I only occasionally catch sight, sports now and then a superb satin cloak at the Opera or Grace Church, after which she lies by for a week's recruit. A thick partition is between our rooms, so that only a confused murmur of their altercations reaches my ear. Once, when the hall doors were open, I caught a few words very sharply uttered, such as, "satin cloaks," "avenue rides," "livery bills," "Stewart's," "my money," "breaking heart," "such a wife," ending, so far as I could judge, in the conquest and humiliation of my "tasteful" neighbor.

The old gentleman above stairs goes to bed regularly at nine, before which he reads in a loud, nasal tone, a passage from the Psalms. He is a quiet, good-hearted old gentleman, who has seen the city growth, he tells me, for fifty years past. He never went out of town further than Newark, where he has a brother residing; yet he sometimes gives me very wholesome advice, and often much valuable information about old families and localities of the town. He takes maccoboy snuff out of a box ornamented with the head of Washington, and turns up his nose at what he calls the "fippy-foppery" of the day. I find that, on many points, we are capitally agreed ; and though he shakes his head at the French poets which are in my library-case, he approves highly my good sense in cherishing an old family copy of Scott's Bible.

The nieces are tidy, prim girls, who are completing their education, by reading French phrase books, Paradise Lost, a pamphlet on Etiquette, and Tupper's Proverbial Philosophy, which they declare to be "sweet." They express, as sensible girls should, who know little or nothing of the matter, a great contempt for the Opera, and most of the fashionable amusements. Yet I observe, that they are always very earnest in their inquiries as to how the house was made up, and about the dresses of the ladies ; and if they can draw me into a little town gossip about the somewhat notorious occupants of particular boxes, they seem delighted with their success. And I once knew them to walk the whole length of the street, in the hope of seeing the Opera troupe, as it came out from rehearsal. They are devoted readers of the Lady's Book, and Mother's Magazine, though very anxious to get an occasional look at the Home Journal, which the tasteful gentleman sometimes purchases ; though the aunt and the old gray-haired lodger persist in condemning it as silly, gossiping trash.

They occasionally walk Broadway in their best hats, to admire the cloaks and mantillas, and yet will talk very earnestly in condemnation of the foolish extravagance of town-ladies. Though they make bold to decry the rules of fashion, and to inveigh against the pursuit of particular, foolish fancies, I find them very ready to suggest to me my short-comings in matters of town etiquette, and they have latterly hinted at some changes of dress, which they are kind enough to say would quite set me up on Broadway, and give me a creditable position at the concerts. My age enables me to bear this very composedly; and further, to crack occasional jokes with them about matrimony, and affairs of gallantry, at which they blush, and affect to be very angry—but are very sure to pardon me, after an incredibly short probation.

Upon the whole, they are quiet, well-disposed girls, who would not make it a material objection to a lover, that he was an Opera-goer, or a little of a Roué: withal, they are small talkers, and do not play the piano.

As you will readily believe, my life passes in such lodgings in the most quiet way imaginable;

and between the old-fashioned talk of the gray-haired lodger, and the dashing conversation of the tasteful gentleman, added to the every-day observations of the demure nieces, I am forming very rapidly a pretty set of conclusions about the classes to which they respectively belong.

But these are by no means all the acquaintances of whose observations I can avail myself; and I shall introduce you, from time to time, to others of wholly different mettle. I shall only excite your curiosity now, by saying that one is a play-actor, —another, a sexton of a fashionable church,—a third is an officer high in the annals of the police, —a fourth is a keen lawyer, one of whose eyes is worth most men's two, —a fifth is a kind and gossiping old lady, who knows half the scandal of the town, with whom I am frequently treated to a drive along the Bloomingdale road, much to the astonishment of the girl lodgers, and of the tasteful gentleman. Still another is a prim clergyman, who, though he is not an Opera-goer, has yet a good ear for a fiddle, and a very delicate eye for mantillas or shoe-ties.

If the mails are true, you will smoke your Tuesday's cigar over this paper; and if you are the friend I take you for, you will look each successive week, with no little curiosity, for the continuance of my observations upon Life in Town.

Though the LORGNETTE is set at the head of my page, you need not suppose that I shall forbear taking an occasional squint, with my naked eye, either above or below; and though I shall sign this TIMON, you must not think, my dear Fritz, that I have entered any Trophonian Cave, or that I cannot, when the humor takes me, play the Merry Andrew, with the gayest of the Town wits.

TIMON.

JAN. 30. NEW-YORK. NO. 2.

Ce sont partout des sujets de satire,
Et comme spectateur, ne puis-je pas en rire ?
ECOLE DES FEMMES.

ANOTHER week has gone by, my dear Fritz, in which the town has been full of its Carnival festivities. Cheeks that were rosy in the opening of the winter, are losing, I see, a little of their vermilion; and the heavy velvet visites, in this spring-like season, are worn with a languid air.

I little thought, in penning my last, that its revelations would betray me; you can judge then of my surprise in being accosted, only two days after its appearance, with the brusque salutation; "*Allons donc, mon cher Timon!*"

It seems that my portraits of the tasteful gentleman and the girls, had been recognized by an acquaintance who sometimes passes an evening at my chambers, over a quiet cigar and a brandy toddy. I have cautioned him, however, against any revelations, and shall now feel myself at liberty to avail myself of his suggestions. He is more of a cynic than myself; and indeed, he is so harsh at times, that I shall feel bound to temper his youthful extravagances, by the coolness and sobriety of my superior years.

This acquaintance, whom I shall call at his own suggestion, Tophanes, being an abbreviation of the old Greek Aristophanes, is a shrewd observer of some eight-and-twenty, well made, of cheerful temperament, city-bred, and has been these four or five years living on the town—by which I mean, that with no ostensible employment, he has yet various occupations, and the best of all professions, for a town-liver—that of passing time agreeably.

He may be frequently seen in an arm-chair, at the head of one of the tables in the reading-room of the Society Library; but I have observed, that while seeming to read, his eye is running over the groups that come every morning to devour the newspapers, and he is summing up in his own mind an estimate of the various characters which make up the company. He follows the same habit in the street, and will watch passers-by, with the careless way of the world, while not an action, or movement will escape his observation. He can tell the daintiness of every lady's waist that he passes, and can furnish a critique upon every bonnet and its trimmings. He knows the name of every belle, and how long she has been upon the town; he has always at hand a description of the peculiar charms of each, whether they lie in figure, in step, in eye, in color, or in money. He can tell to a nicety, by a glance at any one of our ball-room beauties, whether she be *fanée*, *blasée*, or *passée;* he has even, in his time, kept a little note-book, in which he has entered the names of the prominent belles of the day, arranged under various headings, such as—

First Class Belles,
Watering-place Belles,
Second-rate Belles,
New Brighton Belles,
Traveled Belles,
Belles Accessible,
Doubtful Belles,
Stout Belles, and
Eccentric Belles.

Against these, in the true spirit of the Baconian

philosophy, he has entered sundry figures and calculations,—made estimates in a column at the side of the page, and occasionally enlivened the inventory with *pleasant descriptive* paragraphs, and has even given at length the distinguishing characteristics of each species of belle. You will surely agree with me that he is an auxiliary worth having; and when I get upon the topic, I shall very likely make free use of his observations.

His advice to me was most characteristic; nor do I reckon it without value.

"My dear fellow," said he, taking up the yellow pamphlet in his hand, "you are too dainty; you are shy of the mark; you are staving off the very matter which you ought to souse into at once. Set yourself at work upon the elements of our town-society; unravel them, test them, paint them. Dip into this strange Opera-going business, and the puerilities of the coxcomb life. Dish up the Polka for a dinner, and give us bon-bons for dessert. As for the church, the books, and the politicians, they will all come in good time.

"Do you think," said he, turning upon me suddenly, "that you could cultivate a moustache?"

"And why?" said I, stroking my lip and chin.

"Simply because it might be worth a thousand a-year to you, saying nothing of a reversion."

This was a new idea to me, Fritz; you know that in my day, I have worn hair enough upon my face to hide my blushes, even beside the Governor of Comorn, or the prettiest artist of the town. But all this I set down to youthful exuberance, and the careless habit of travel; I thought it a duty to my Christian brotherhood, to wear now, in the calm and quiet of life, at least a Christian physiognomy. Tophanes explained the matter to me, thus:

"My dear fellow," said he, assuming the air of a patron, "you must see a little more of town life than will come under your eye in these retired quarters; your name is not particularly tonnish, though it has fortunately a slight foreign air (my great-grandfather, from whom I inherited it, was a Fleming); you don't keep a 'drag' or a 'milord;' your seat at the Opera is an humble one; you are not even boarder at the New-York Hotel; you have not the entrée at Madame——, (naming a leader of the exquisite ton); you are a little passé; you have nothing particularly distingué in your air; your dress is country made; you have not, that I know of, been guilty of any little pretty pardonable crimes against society; you have not fought a duel, except a sham one, with broad-swords, behind the old ruin at Heidelberg; you can't very well, at your time of life, get credit for a *liason* with one of the Opera troupe,—so, my dear fellow, there is no hope for you, but—a moustache !"

I saw at once the justice of his observations, and determined to consider the matter. I wished, however, first to look about me, and see what manner of men were wearing these very essential appendages, and when my observation shall be complete,—of which, my dear Fritz, you shall have a full report, —I will tell you plainly what decision the circumstances force upon me. Meantime, with the aid of my friend Tophanes (with whom we will smoke a pipe together on your first visit), I give you this little sketch of the city growth of a fashionable man.

—

THE FASHIONABLE MAN

Homunculus.—Passim.

You know him first at an age varying from fifteen to twenty, by his very prim, square shirt collar,—by a speckled Joinville tie, a very large-bottomed *pantalon*, a boot that must pinch him execrably, and a hat set the slightest possible bit on one side of his head. He usually walks Broadway, at this stage of incipiency, arm-in-arm with a companion, for he has seen cuts of this mode of procedure, in the high-life illustrations to Dickens' works; and he may sometimes be seen swaggering with a very bold air, and very flat cigar, out of such corner oyster shops as those of Florence, or Sherwood. At this age, too, he talks in a very glib style of the ladies,—their dress and tournure ;—he mentions very familiarly by their first names, certain dashing specimens who ride in hackney cabs, and who walk always unattended ; and he affects punches, made very strong. He boldly tips the wink to the bar-maid, at such genteel places as the Madison House—sips, and pulls up his shirt collars with a jaunty air, and sometimes will sit down to a quiet rubber of whist, in the back parlor.

His mamma, who wishes to restrain his out of door indulgences, by breeding in him a love for polished society, invites ladies of undoubted respectability to her house, and our young master of the Joinville tie commences early practice of the gallantries of the drawing-room. His dancing education is not neglected, and he soon gets a name with the visiting ladies, for a very pleasant handling of their forms in the Redowa. He cultivates assiduously some elder acquaintance at the New-York Club, so that his card and address come to be familiarly known to the purveyor of the establishment, and will get by merest accident upon such lady's lists, as are made up from the club roll.

Our nero patronizes (that is his word) a fashionable tailor, and sets off a coat, by dint of slight wadding, capitally well. His etiquette in the dressing-room at the balls, is highly careless; and he draws on his gloves, and adjusts his hair after the last patterns of established town gentlemen. If no prominent fashionable sciou be found in the dressing-room, he assumes quite an air, and talks in very gay humor, and with dashing familiarity of the ladies below; but if he espies an old Nestor of the balls, he shrinks into comparative quietude, and carefully observes the action and deportment of his senior.

His dancing is easy and piquant, and he finds without difficulty dashing lady partners, who grown a little anxious on the score of their own age, are very willing to commute the stock of years, by balancing the Polka with a boy.

His talk is necessarily somewhat juvenile; but he has a carefully prepared round of critiques on Bertucca and Forti, picked up at the clubs; and on weather topics, he manifests an insouciance and freedom, that show him to be a perfect master of the subject. He sometimes even ventures upon the fine arts, and has cultivated certain ecstasies of expression about the Greek Slave, and such like measures of the town taste, which would be worthy of an established belle, or the columns of the Sunday Mercury.

Oldish men, and such ladies as have rather an unfortunate reputation for good sense, set off with a spice of satire, he is careful to avoid; he sneers at their ill-nature, only because their irony is too strong for his brain.

With his fellows, perhaps he will affect a sporting turn; he will read very assiduously the Spirit of the Times,—he will have a shooting jacket made with a world of pockets, and will sometimes take it with him, on a trip to a summer watering-place; but only wears it occasionally of a morning, when he is sure no sportsmen are by; he will stuff a pocket with pressed Regalias, and regret that game is so scarce. He talks in very knowing tones of quail and partridge, of Greener guns and Frank Forrester, and is supplied with all the sporting *on dits*. He discourses too about trout-fishing, and Alfred's tackle, very much as one of the falsettos in the Papal choir, might talk of deeds of gallantry.

In time, he may come to have a small purplish gathering of hair upon the upper lip, and he consults Cristadoro on the prospects of a full-fledged moustache. Meantime he is rapidly pushing his ventures in the fashionable world; he may even boast of a speaking acquaintance with some one of the Opera troupe of ladies, which he mentions to his friends with a sly leer, as if something were in the wind.

He discards, as he gets on, his Joinville tie ; he observes closely the air of foreign gentlemen at the New-York Hotel, and will presently appear in a stout, heavy "coachman," with huge pearl buttons. He is apt, at this stage, to invite some French gentleman who is living on the town, to a dinner at Delmonico's; and if he can push this venture into a decided familiarity with the foreign representative of manners, he feels himself a made man.

If a literary fancy seizes him, he will cultivate the acquaintance of the musical critics of the newspapers; he accosts them familiarly (when no ladies are in sight) in the corridors of the Opera-house, and will perhaps contribute a letter to the Sunday Herald, or a rejected sonnet to the Evening Mirror. His reading will be variously the Home Journal, the Dispatch, and "all sorts of paragraphs" of the Evening Post; and when he feels braced for really serious work, he will perhaps undertake "a card" in the Courier and Enquirer, a review in the Literary World, a poem in the Tribune, or a chapter in "James' last Novel."

Provided with such stock of literary matter as

this general reading furnishes, he quite astounds the young ladies, who, though very good dancers, do not pretend to be deep; and who smile the prettiest coquetry back, at all his literary disquisitions, disclaiming earnestly the name of blues. He will, however, be rewarded by the very warm looks of book-loving spinsters, and perhaps be invited to a *conversazione*, where if he have a good tongue, and a few tricks of the players, he may establish a tender reputation by a triumphant reading of Romeo and Juliet.

As he grows older, he discards such follies as unworthy the dignity of a man of ton, and as entirely useless in the art of salon conquest. If his means will allow the venture, he will perhaps occasionally drive a showy horse, in very dainty harness, along the Bloomingdale road. At the Opera, he will be provided with a very huge Lorgnette of ebony, or imitation, and will direct it with the coolest composure into a lady's face of the next box; and he will never forget to break out into a rapturous bravo, when a tall critic in the parquette, or Madame —— gives the concerted signal for applause. And if one of the troupe appears in unreasonably short petticoats, he is sure to level his glass at her, with a most obstinate gaze, and crack some very touching jokes, which make the lady he is with, blush to her eyes—unless indeed, she is lately returned from "abroad," and is gazing as earnestly as he, sighing at the prurient modesty of American women. In this last case indeed, she will have the advantage of him in audacity, and will talk as coolly of the shape of Signora's legs, as if it were the daintiest imaginable topic for a quiet breakfast chat.

And our hero gains from such encouragement, at the hands of one who has formed her taste for morals, and her moral of taste, at Paris, a new step in his life of fashion; and at his next *soirée*, he will repeat the ladies compliments of Signora, until his dancing partner blushes again. He is now arrived at a ripe stage; and if Mesdames So-and-so do not invite him to their balls, it is because they do not know that a most agreeable talent for ready and piquant conversation, has been added to his graceful accomplishment in the waltz. He now assumes patronizing airs toward the younger members of his class, and condescendingly offers to present them at the reception of his lady friends.

A little of the reputation of the *roué*, will at this stage add an agreeable spice to his character; and an intrigue, coyly hinted at, with some married lady, and offering topic for luxurious chit-chat in fashionable boudoirs, will be very sure to give him the entrée to the houses of such "leaders of the ton" as have hitherto smiled contemptuously at his pretensions. Old ladies of fashion, grown fat on drawing-room applause, and luxurieus riding, will taste with as mush relish as a dish of game, grown rank, the luscious flattery dropping from the lips of a man who has so successfully won his honors.

Now he may count securely on being made manager of watering-place balls, and will be beset by mothers of doubtful position, to take pity on their daughters. He is looked up to by all barbers and head-waiters, as a man of immense consideration; and he will walk Broadway with the air of one who feels that little remains to be learned, and that his character is beyond criticism. He is a club-man; and if his cards are well played, and a lofty ambition spurs him on, he may have the honor of figuring in the newspapers as one of a committee to give a public dinner, or to aid in a city reception, or to do honor to a distinguished ballet-dancer.

Higher than this, it is hardly possible for the man of fashion to go. He is now become the Achilles of the street, and the Apollo of the boudoir. If his funds diminish, or his coiffeur hints at need of a hair dye, he turns his thoughts to marriage; and presently all the ladies of a certain age are bewitched to secure him. Not because he has fortune, or much mental calibre, or because he is a man to turn the world upside down, or to make a figure on the Exchange, or in the courts, or because possessed of any really intrinsic grace of character,—but then he is such a charming man,—so very agreeable,—such a funny man,—so elegant,—with such handsome eyes,—or such a moustache,—and then he *polks* so prettily,—in short, he is such a dear love of a man!

And as for the stories about him and Madame So-and-So, there can surely be nothing in them; he is so audible in his responses at Grace Church, and such a friend of Doctor ——; it must be all envy; but perhaps Madame So-and-So courted him; and then he is so kind; and even if he did, how penitent he must be; and what a delightful thing to win him back to the paths of virtue! And the fair apologist, very strong in her love of mercy and purity, and shedding religious tears of hope, throws herself back upon her luxurious lounge, and gets a new lesson of Christian charity and morals, out of that dear Catholic story of the Lady Alice.

But the Papa has perhaps in this arrangement, a keener eye to prudence, than to piety. He is very earnest in his inquiries about stocks, and expectations; and is anxious to know of what timber the fashionable man may be built. A moustache, though a very good recommendation to my lady's boudoir, or balls, is not, he shrewdly thinks, so taking on exchange; nor is it altogether the readiest passport to the confidence and inveiglement of such clients as manifest a decided wish that their business should have attention. White kids appear very prettily in the handling of a LORGNETTE, but they must be cast to manage the execution of a deed, or to draft a bill of exchange. The pretty babble about the Dusseldorf, or the tenor of Forti, may do very well to win a weak lady, but it will not have very great weight with a jury. Our man of fashion has then one position up-town, and quite another in Wall street: among the women, he passes for a man; and among the men, he passes for a woman.

If in this emergency of his life, his funds absolutely fail, he may possibly find friends, who for the credit of the family, will subscribe for him an annuity, payable until he shall secure an heiress. He is now obliged to cut his old acquaintances of the Opera troupe, and hushes up his reputation for intrigue, except so much as shall find its way by friendly lips, to the ears of his victim. For in this quarter, no acquaintance can do him worse service, than by sneering at his past gallantries, as sheer affectations; and he may safely say with the lover, in the French Comedy: *Je ne demandais pas à être mauvais sujet; mais, maintenant que c'est reconnu et établi, il ne faut rien dire! Car en m'ôtant mes torts, on m'ôterais tous mes avantages.*

However, he is regular at church, and affects thoughtfulness, for he is put perhaps, by some form-loving mamma, upon probation.

What a changed man!—whispers the delighted Fredonia; and presently, from a rake, our fashionable man has become a husband. He has married a plump five thousand a-year, a delicate complexion, a great deal of whalebone and bustle, a smattering of French talk, whole reams of poetic sentiment, and an incalculable quantity of new novels.

He can now take a box at the Opera, and ride to Grace Church; he can wink at the sexton, shake hands with the parson, and utter his responses as audibly as he chooses. He cuts his poor acquaintances of the club, and doesn't let his country cousins know his town address. He drops pennies into the parish box, wrapped in dingy brown paper, which resembles old bank bills, and passes with pious, middle-aged ladies, for a worthy and charitable Christian. He gives parties, but he does not pay his grocer's bill.

His wife has expectations, and he takes her rheumatic uncle out to ride, and presses upon him his

THE FASHIONABLE MAN.

poor cigars, and is very urgent that he should come to dine with him, when he knows him to be laid up with an attack of the gout. He sends bouquets, and valentines, anonymously, but in his own handwriting, to his wife's rich aunt. He employs a fashionable physician, and doesn't venture into Wall street. He goes to play billiards at the club, and tells his wife he has business with his lawyer. He goes to parties, and waltzes with the youngest girls in the room. He figures on committees for public balls, and wears white rosette; he consults his wife's complexion in the purchase of dress, and drapery, and has long and serious interviews with his tailor. He subscribes to a morning and evening paper, and to the Home Journal; and he has his arms cut upon a signet ring. He reads general news in de Trobriand's Revue, and the religious news, in the directions for church service, of the prayer-book.

He talks with his clergyman about church architecture,—with his lawyer about marriage settlements,—with his wife about the last party, and with his lady friends about velvet cloaks, and the new third fiddler of the orchestra.

At this stage, he may be reckoned firmly and fairly a leader of the ton; and he has only to show himself liberal, to have his name heralded, or his likeness cut for the Sunday Mercury; and very especial services may secure to him the honor of a statuette in the shop windows of the town.

His moneyed character is of course understood to be beyond impeachment; or if some unfortunate developments of an irksomely keen morning paper, should make his name and note discredited on 'Change, he has only to appear in a dignified, exculpatory card, drafted by his lawyer,—to withdraw his funds at the bank,—make over the result of a few private transactions to his wife,—contract a few debts of honor, from such friends as will not bother him for pay, and live upon his wife's charity,—another gorgeous, and dinner-loving martyr to town speculation, and to bitter tongues.

This, as I am assured by my friend Tophanes, is a fair representation of the usual growth; but the exceptions are very various, and the grades of fashionable men are very numerous. There are, for instance,—the fashionable beaux, the fashionable street-men, the fashionable authors, the fashionable *roués*, the fashionable merchants, the fashionable respectables, the fashionable defaulters, the fashionable grocers, and the fashionable doctors. And when I come to detail their characteristics at length, they will, I am sure, my dear Fritz, amuse you wonderfully.

I shall not venture to give you thus early any sketch of the fashionable development in the women; for since it is a more delicate matter, I must make my observation a little finer, and have a few more quiet talks with my old lady friend, who as I told you, sometimes indulges me with a ride in her britska. And I may further say, that any advices in regard to this topic, from genteel young women, of good taste and connections, will be very gladly received. My friend Tophanes, who is an up-town liver, has kindly volunteered to take charge of any such communications as may be left for John Timon, at the counter of Henry Kernot, bookseller. He has, moreover, tendered his services to make personal calls, between the hours of twelve and three, upon such ladies as have anything of a special nature to communicate. (Tophanes moves in "top society," and he will engage to call, in blue coat with brass buttons, yellow gloves, and a jaunty-looking hack; and if desired, the coachman will wear a gilt band around his hat.)

I am determined to spare no pains to make my portraits of town life, true to the spirit of the times; so that any future historian of our social growth, may find in these humble papers, the material suited to his purpose.

Timon.

FEB. 7. NEW-YORK. NO. 3.

"It is the same vanity, the same folly, and the same vice, only appearing different, as viewed through the glass of fashion. In a word, all mankind are a ——."—GOLDSMITH.

You will be amused to learn, my dear Fritz, that a city paper has set you down as a respectable maiden aunt of a certain poor literary jobber, to whom has been ascribed the authorship of these papers. I do not doubt but that you would become the petticoats as well as any Catholic Sister of the "People I have met;" still I feel bound to enter a *caveat* against such wanton and gratuitous metamorphose of your dignity and sex.

As for the alleged authorship,—notwithstanding the allegation is supported by "undoubted signs,"—I have only to say that the editors must set their wits at work anew. It is certainly not a little singular, that after having plainly told the public, that my name was wholly unknown, gentlemen should persist in ascribing the work to persons of acknowledged experience. Will not the dear Critics believe, that a plain and simple observer may use a pen with some little adroitness, although he has not dipped into the muddy Bethesda of city literature? May not a man speak out honestly his sentiments, and detail the pleasant passages of his town-life, without being set down as one of the old brood of inordinate and pretentious scribblers? Is there anything in the nature of the thing, that forbids the propriety, or the truth of my claim? Will not the kind gentlemen—the bell-wethers of the sheep-flock—who have in their keeping the literary interests of the town, suffer a quiet fellow to have a word for himself, but they must forthwith credit his speculations to some of their own kith and kin?

As for the honor they do me, deeply sensible as I am of its importance, I must yet entreat their forbearance in the bestowal; it hurts my modesty, to say nothing of my character.

It seems that not a few curious *smelfungi*, misled, perhaps, by the taking figure of the cover, have anticipated in the LORGNETTE a sort of *duodecimo*

Judy, with its grinning conceits; they are as much mistaken as if they were to look for classic acting at the Broadway Theatre, or for a conscience among the City Fathers. Those earnest for such funny delicacies, I would commend to the Chatham Theatre, an old file of Yankee Doodle, and a pewter mug of ale; and with these helps, I feel quite sure that they may turn them out, as plentifully, and of as good quality, as any at the bar of the Jefferson Lunch, or among the city items of the Commercial.

TOWN CELEBRITIES.

"If you wish to make people stare by doing better than others, why make them stare till they stare their eyes out?"—JOHNSON.

I SHOULD give you a poor idea, Fritz, of the winter life in town, if I did not keep you advised from week to week of the celebrities of the time; yet they come up so fast, that it will be very hard to tell how they gain such character, and harder still, to tell how they lose it. But we are a quick-working people, and do these things at very short order; while, you know, in the old states of Europe, it takes a long time for either man, woman, or child, to become any way famous. There the most extraordinary men may move about without a procession of gapers; and a Lolah Montes may take her dish of coffee at a public table, without so much as a single man being choked with his roll at the sight.

This is not the way we do things in our town. Nothing out of the common course can happen but there arises a tremendous buzz, which carries knowledge of it to all the salons of the town, and to every loge of the Opera. Not a man above the capacity of country Judge, or skipper of a coasting schooner, can arrive upon the island, but he is announced in the gossiping papers under the head of personal movements; and I do not believe that a man could kiss his wife in the street without its forming a nucleus for a "mysterious circumstance" in an evening journal, or that a lady could rupture her lacings, without its being chronicled in the Express, under head of "Casualties."

The ingenious de Tocqueville would have found a reason for this itch of multiplying the marvelous, in the character of our institutions, and in the absence, throughout our social system, of all established and time-honored celebrities. We must have something near us to wonder at and admire, and if the State does not give us the means, why our own fancies will. Hence it is that mountebanks of all classes and characteristics, are passing before us, and growing in a breath into celebrities.

Tophanes, who is *au courant* of such matters, has frequently diverted me, by pointing out, upon the street, the lions of the day. There, for instance,—he will tell me,—goes a woman who is well known for having the prettiest ankles in the town, and who is remarkable for a partiality to damp pavements. Another is known for her artistic arrangement of dress, and has even been honored, under a feigned name, with a complimentary paragraph, under head of "things talked of" in the Home Journal. A third has given a magnificent ball, with which the town talk, from that of the prim nieces in the attic, to that of a distinguished French reviewer, has been busy for a week. Mention in the last-named quarter has, of course, established reputation beyond all attempt at cavil.

A fourth, who is a prim gentleman in very shaggy coat, is pointed out to you as the hero of every salon; and if he but add to this claim a certain celebrity in the Rackett court, or the authorship of a few sonnets, he will be gazed at admiringly by all the young ladies upon town. A fifth, is a millionaire, or son of a millionaire, who has a hundred sly fingers and beaming eyes directed toward him, whenever he shows himself upon the walk. A sixth, will be named and noted as the hero of some little piquant intrigue, which the dear ladies name always with a Christian shudder, and such fond sigh of regret as might win a Joseph. Another, is some blooming author, or artist, who, by dint of newspaper mention, has grown Raphaelesque in celebrity, and who wears his honors like a mountain. I do not mean to say, Fritz, that these are characters whose fame has reached you, for their celebrity, unfortunately, blossoms and fades within the limits of the city. If they were to migrate, they might become lions in small country towns for a season; but it is to be feared, that without the ambrosia of town Deism, they would soon sink to the level of ordinary men.

Indeed, so determined is the disposition to build up easy celebrities, that I have had my fears, lest some of the paper limners, who are the most prying, inquisitive fellows you can imagine—should get wind of my box at the Opera, since I am a stranger, and very indefatigable with my glass—and serve me up in a paragraph under some such dainty head as "Riff Raff," or "Floatings By." Indeed, what with my rustic air, huge lorgnette, and bald head, I think I should cut rather a pretty figure in a statuette. And if Heaven were to spread before me the snare of a town marriage, I should expect to find all my better feelings harrowed up by some such announcement as this :—" We understand that a buxom old country gentleman, Mr. John Timon, led yesterday to the altar the young and blooming Miss Euphemia Trymen. The ceremony was performed in Grace Church, and the powerful and sonorous voice of the distinguished Doctor added powerfully to the interest of the stirring occasion. Several carriages were in attendance, among which we noticed a few of the tasteful equipages of our leaders of fashion."

Foreigners in general may, so far as I have observed, be reckoned among the town celebrities. A German, with his guttural sounds, and with his taste in music, which, by dint of foreign terms, can be very well assumed, is almost certain of being hunted down, and bagged by all the good-natured celebrity mongers. And if he can scrape a fiddle daintily, or talk, with his eyes rolling to heaven, about Goethe, or cultivate a Faust intensity of look, he will be in demand all over the town by German loving young ladies,—and all this, notwithstanding he may drink all the small beer in the world, or smoke the filthiest of Meerschaums. It is of but little account what name or position he may have held in the Fatherland: we *democratize* with a vengeance, where a distingué, sandy whisker is in the case; and our autocrats can open their doors to the veriest valet, if his lingual acquirements and *naïve* foreign air will but make him a taking card in the salon.

As for the Frenchman, though now between the valorous Poussin and the long-faced Bonaparte, a little under the weather, yet a good polka education, delicate perfumes well laid on, and a roundly-uttered "*superbe*," and "*magnifique*," in a lady's ear, will do for him vast execution. And as for a genuine Cockney, in exceedingly sharp shirt collars, straight-brimmed hat, and plaid tights, who mouths his words, and says,—"I de-say," and "it's very odd," and "nice person," and who talks easily about "Victy," and the "Duke,"—he will bewitch half the women of the town. And if he can manage to drop a compliment, not too clumsily contrived, into the ear of some *respectable*, established lady, who doats upon herself, her suppers, and her equipage, he will be heralded presently in the town gossip, as a "distinguished son of Albion," with supposed acquirements enough to make him a ten days' wonder. Of course, if a shrewd fellow, his acquaintance at home will be all be-duked, and be-duchessed, and he will prove a rare trump for such ladies as turn up their noses at "money," and who have a keen scent for "blood."

But all these have latterly been cast in the shade

THE HUNGARIANS

by the Hungarian exiles; among which were the valiant little Demoiselle Jagello, and Governor Ujhazy, whose names the whole town has learned to pronounce, by aid of the philological developments of a morning paper. Now nothing in the world is more proper than to welcome these poor fellows; and nothing more generous than Stetson's kind bounty in giving them a home. But they have been fêted, and visited; and the stout little curmudgeon of a Governor drugged with dinners, and Mademoiselle tolled out to town balls; and important committees have been busy making up for us a set of celebrities as large as the Mexican conquerors. They have been sent for to make a house at the Opera, and have proved grand capital, not only for Senator Seward, but for aspiring ladies who give thin *soirées*. Would it not be well for them to secure, as standard lions for the season, a score or two of those who are now on their way from Hamburg?

Now if the Governor, who is a stern old countryman, with a long grizzled beard like a Hebrew, would take honest advice, I would caution him against celebrity mongers, and urge upon him a quiet life, and a careful look-out for his estates at home; which, if they pass from him in the lion's division of the spoil, he had better renew somewhere in the

West, and bend that sturdy back of his to work upon American soil, and that brave soul to the appreciation and advancement of the American State.

As for Mademoiselle, who is a brisk, snug-built, dark-eyed little maid, they have made all manner of paragraphs about her shape, her tears, and her war-dress—in short, they have married her to town celebrity ; and though it is a far better match for her, than if she had married the best of the celebrity mongers, yet it will make for her an unquiet home, and will give her but flimsy altar-gods for her hearth-stone.

Another poor victim they have tried to make of a splendid violinist, ushered in by a blast of town trumpets, and the taking announcement of a weekly journal that he was a "handsome young fellow." The town ladies were naturally bewitched to see the charming Remeyni, who, though scarce out of his teens, had the sense to perceive the lure, and as Tophanes informs me, has escaped the martyrdom.

But the Hungarian fever, thanks to the stupidity of that lover of monarchs and the London Times—Mr. Bowen, has become almost chronic; and we hear of respectable young men and women, sane on other matters, who have actually taken to study of the Magyar dialect, and talk of some such redeeming pilgrimages to the banks of the Danube, as crazy Southey once plotted to the wilds of Missouri. In all the *bals costumês* the Hungarian costume is just now carrying the day, even against a Buena Vista hussar coat, or the lace trimmings of a *Debardeur*. Street mountebanks are wearing Hungarian caps; the Hungarian balsam is in new demand; and Miss Lawson (Tophanes is my authority), who divides, with the Home Journal, the honors of being Pythoness of modes, is about to offer to the enchanted town a Jagello hat! The next step will be a *Weehazy* polka, and a *Weehazy* beard, which, if they be duly chronicled in the Express, and countenanced by her Grace, Madame J——, and deftly dished into an oily paragraph, by the Journal that dishes such things so well, will become the established order of the city.

As for native growth, now that the Mexican war is fairly over (which, as I am told, crowded the town with heroes), the ways of achieving a really available celebrity are reducible to some one of these:—by getting, or seeming to get, inordinately rich; by giving a ball so splendid that it shall not lack notice even in the staid columns of a *Revue;* by writing a stupid book (if I said letters, you might condemn me for an aspirant!); by newspaper mention under head of "Personal Movements," or the committal of some extraordinary absurdity ; by defaulting to the tune of some really clever sum ; by making a dinner speech, or getting drunk at the balls ; by running away with an heiress, or arriving as "bearer of dispatches ;" and finally, by being candidate for, or recipient of a public office.

There are many of them so important as to be worthy of a separate paper ; and I shall go on now to note only the casual and accidental celebrities which have fallen under notice.

An Opera ball, one of which has lately miscarried, owing to an unfortunate clash of jealousies, might be made, by a little dexterous management, a thorough celebrity. I have the authority of my neighbor, the tasteful gentleman, for saying that the only one of the winter was quite *recherché ;* and he has kindly offered to interest himself with the managers, for securing me a ticket to such others as may be in store. He tells me that it is strictly understood between Mr. Maretzek and the tasteful managers, that no *parvenus* are to be admitted ; and as I am quite anxious to see the pure ton sifted of all riff-raff, parvenu rubbish, I shall certainly avail myself of his kindness. It is true I have had my misgivings about his own title to the floor ; but it appears that he is intimate with the chief of the orchestra, and has performed some private service of a delicate nature, for a gentleman prominent on the committee; moreover, he wears a very respectable moustache, a jaunty-setting blue coat with brass buttons, and an air of easy indifference, so that he passes without challenge.

Some of the "old families," as he calls them, have turned up their noses at these public balls; but he hints that it is out of sheer jealousy, and that they are fast being overtopped by the ton of the Opera-house. And he went on to say, that the manners of such were altogether rusty and stiff, not brilliant enough for the times, and that they must soon sink into oblivion. I am inclined to think that he is more than half correct; and if the old Dutchmen do not take warning—add a new cape to their coachmen's coat, trick out their daughters in more dashing cloaks, buy a seat at Grace Church, (though Dutch Reform stock may rise a little with the cross of the Fifth Avenue *Meeting-House*,) abuse Forti, subscribe to de Trobriand's Revue, and the LORGNETTE, they will be very sure to lose caste.

There are not a few diminutive celebrities of the balls—people who get a name for constant attendance, or for a particular dance; and I remember quite a young gentleman with a little down upon his lip, carefully turned up at the ends, who was pointed out by my friend Tophanes, as an extraordinary prodigy in this last way. He seemed to have a due sense of his lion state, albeit his mane was not of very robust growth, and seemed as thoroughly satisfied with his celebrity, as if it had been gained by the invention of a steam-engine, or a patent elastic boot shank.

I don't mean, dear Fritz, to affect the cynic, in making invidious comparisons, and by throwing ridicule on the favorites of the balls. Each phase of life has its brilliancies, and each pursuit its celebrities ; and there is no reason in the world why our heroes of the polka should not wear their honors of the pump, as serenely, and gaily, as the first whip at Astley's his success upon the box—as Celeste her verdicts of applause at the Lyceum, or as our new-fledged writers their sprouting and hot-bed glories.

The lady celebrities of the ball-room are distinguishable sometimes by gracefulness in the dance, and sometimes by a most delectable familiarity. Why, if our old flame Amy, of *bal masqué* memory, were to cling to you in the waltz with such languishing and tender air as belongs to some of our salon dancers, you would find yourself doubting if she were as honest as she seemed.

Only fancy to yourself, Fritz, a tall girl with shoulders bare to the lower edge of decorum,—your arm clasped round her waist well bound up,—her hand lying hard upon your shoulder, and her head sometimes reposing on it, so that her head-dress tickles your chin as you whirl in the dance, and a round eye full of a luxurious languor looking up at you from the faint head! To tell you the truth, it would do honor to the *Chaumière*.

My old lady-friend the dowager explained this to me, however, as a pleasant eccentricity of the dancer; and supported her statement by pointing out to me presently the same individual, in the act of borrowing a gentleman's handkerchief to wipe the perspiration from her neck! The town is certainly on the gain in these matters; the old prurient modesty of our day is gone by; and we may expect to see, in a winter or two, some of these eccentric characters appearing in satin breeches. Indeed, I would by no means vouch for the fact, that they have not enjoyed particular *divertisements* of the sort, before a select company of gentlemen, already.

I cannot help noticing in this connection, though they hardly rank among the celebrities, the great number of small fry, who swarm at the balls. The age of school-boys seems to have utterly gone by; and you will find little witlings in straight sharp collars talking robustly of polking, and balls, at an age when, judging from their chin and brain, they should be busy with their Latin readers and Columbian class-books. And if you fall to talking with a hoydenish miss, or decayed spinster, about Rossi, or the new tenor, (for these are safe topics) you will find yourself supplanted by some little beardless fellow, who scarce comes up to your shoulder, and who yet insists with all the gravity of a man, upon the next *polk*, with your belle!

It used to be the order, that men should have the gain of a year or two upon the ladies; but the order seems now reversed, and a boy in his teens is reckoned a fit partner for a woman of a score. Whether the ladies have degenerated, or the youngsters gained four years upon them in wit, since our day, I have not yet observed enough to determine correctly.

Another sort of celebrity at the balls is the diner-out, who is heavy with Port and Champagne, and stupified with a new lift at the punch-bowl. He quite shocks sensitive girls by the boldness of his dance, and thinks it a pretty play to reel like a Bacchante through the waltz. In this matter, New-York fashionables decidedly take the lead of the rest of the civilized world; in most quarters such unfortunate diners-out would be politely shown the door; but it is by no means certain that here, it does not add to a gentleman's attractions.

Here and there you may meet with a traveled lady who becomes a pretty subject for salon celebrity. She wears an air of most captivating impudence, and pronounces the names of a great many foreign towns unexceptionably, even to the Gaelic guttural in Munich. She wears gloves from Boivín's in the Rue de la Paix, and hopes she shall never be obliged to wear any others : she subscribes to the Courrier des Etats-Unis, and criticises the American translations of French authors. She drops her cards about town, dating from the Rue Lavoisier, or de Lille, and leaves a regret with the servant, that she has no American cards about her. She talks in a hurried, broken, epigrammatic way of Paris shops and *soirées*,—assumes that air of easy languor, which becomes the elegant *faineant*, weary of admiration, and gives such interesting details of city life abroad as dazzle her beardless devotees, but which it is plain to see are picked up from a gossiping French *femme de chambre*. It is wonderful how much pretty talk of travel, and scandal of Paris life, can be accumulated from the morning chats with a little piquant grisette ; and if any ambitious conversationist is desirous of lighting up her evenings with richer foreign tattle than can be gathered from any "scissorings from foreign files," there could scarce be a happier method hit upon than to import for private service, a middle-aged, faded, Paris *femme de chambre.*

Our foreign celebrity criticises in *ex cathedra* style the dresses of the town, and makes modest young women, who are simply respectable, very uneasy in their simplicity. If a friend questions the propriety of certain extravagances of dress, she meets it with an inimitable toss of the head, that quite sets the matter at rest. Or if some prudent old lady inveighs against a too lavish display of her personal charms,—Pho! has she not seen the dress of the Duchess of So and So, and shall she be taught proprieties in our town?

A young gentleman of 'parts,' and high respectability, will be presented by some middle-aged spinster as a gentleman recently returned from abroad, and possibly a hint will be dropped about superior acquirements, a German university, or a finished education. At all which, the young gentleman of 'parts' adjusts his shirt collar, looks down at his Paris boot, bows graciously, and thinks "it is a fine day." Or if last from England, he coughs "ahem," and says "aye," in affirmation, —clips his words very uncommonly short, and affects a most extraordinary coolness, with which the young ladies are delighted, and think "he is so very gentlemanly." He says that St. Paul's is a fair sort of a church, and also Westminster Abbey, in its way ; and he thinks the Duke of Northumberland has "raything a clever 'ouse" at Charing Cross, but he doesn't think his equipage is the 'thing.'

He intends "going over" again presently to hear Jenny Lind, or to see Cerito. Of course he thinks Truffi is very well in her way, but quite provincial—quite ! As for Paris, which he pronounces inadvertently Paree, he was quite charmed with it —quite ; and he can give a very particular and graphic description of the Hotel Meurice, and such statistics about palaces and gardens, as he has picked up from his valet de place, or Galignani's Guide. Of course he became perfectly familiar with French, and has a practical knowledge of Italian and Spanish ; though it seems to him a confounded affectation to be using these unusual acquirements in company ; for his part, he could not so far forget himself. He can tell some very rich stories about brigands in Italy, which date *about* the time of his visit.

For the matter of Art, he must confess with some pain, that he has not been able to enter our small collections since his return ; but he hopes that after a little further depletion of the foreign habit, he will be sufficiently reduced to enjoy even the Art-Union

Yet he would by no means sneer at our artists—he would not be thought to do so; he thinks they need encouragement, particularly that of men of taste and travel.

He opens a conversation with a new acquaintance, by observing, that upon the whole manners are improving in this country; he sees marks of it, he thinks, all about him,—particularly in the little naked statuettes which he has met with in private parlors; and he does sincerely hope that we shall soon become thoroughly refined in such matters. He doesn't know but the etiquette is as yet a little provincial, but he kindly thinks that its taint will wear off by degrees.

He talks about the London Times, and hopes he shall not lose sight of it; he feels quite an interest in some of the noble families; and says it was rumored as he left *town*, that his acquaintance, the son of the Marquis of So and So, was about to marry the Honorable Juliana Titus.

Drop to him a remark about the weather, and he says he quite likes it—quite the London air; he passed last season in London, and asks if the steamer has arrived. At the hotels he affects the English manner with the waiters—calling them all 'John,' and the porter, 'boots'; or he strikes his tumbler with his fork, and calls out accidentally,

Garçon! and will sometimes forget himself so far, after dinner, as to call the stout Irish chambermaid—*mon petit chat!*

He calls a hack-driver, cabman; and the omnibus drivers, coachmen; he never says cents, but pennies; and sometimes talks of ha'pennies, and calls the Hudson, "Tems." He talks about rectors, and curates, and vicars, and good livings, and says he quite unconsciously found himself praying, the other Sunday, "for Her Most Gracious Majesty, the Queen, and all the Royal Family!"

I fancy, Fritz, that you smile ironically at these learned and accomplished graduates of foreign travel; and your smiles are not ill-timed. And I am half persuaded to cast aside reserve, and my quiet habit of talk, to lash as they deserve these puerile coxcombs, fed on their own vanity, and the tolerance of the town. Yet there are plenty of weak ones—not all of them weak from lack of years—who listen with unction to such conceited babblers, and who fructify this sort of celebrity, by renewing expressions of applause, and studied smiles of adulation.

You are enough of an American, my dear Fritz, though you have wintered in the snows of Petersbourg, and lighted your spring with the delicious glow of a Greek sun rising over the Ægean, to wish for something more earnest, strong, and manly in American life, than will permit the every-day prostration before the social Juggernaut of Europe.

When, in the name of Heaven, are we to have an honest, simple, Republican basis for our socialities, which shall not need, nor ask the meretricious adornments of foreign style, and which shall reject all miserable pilferers of those trappings which belong to the lordly state of the Old World, as incapable of manly intent, and a severe Republican dignity?

The jackdaw may steal peacocks' feathers, but they will not make him an eagle.

TIMON.

FEB. 14. NEW-YORK. NO. 4.

J'en fais un aveu public; je me suis proposé que de representer la vie des hommes telle qu'elle est; a Dieu ne plaise que j'aie eu dessein de désigner quelqu'un en particulier!—LE SAGE.

I AM sorry, Fritz, that my letters to you, written down in the humor of the moment, and containing such observations upon town life and society, as I thought would be agreeable to you to read, should have provoked the condemnation of bearing too great a severity of remark, and of wearing an air of bitterness. I had hoped to be so far sustained by sensible men and women, in ridicule of what all must confess to be worthy of ridicule, as to escape such reproof. You know me well enough, Fritz, to be aware that it is not in my nature to dislike for the sake of disliking, or to sneer, from a habit of sneering.

Is it true, that what all the world reproves in talk, is not to be reproved in print? and that exceptions which are taken every day to particular extravagances, are no sooner made public, and reduced to the point of words, than they change to imputed slanders? I abjure this construction, and the charges which it entails.

A lady of piquant talk will play off the shafts of her wit upon ridiculous usages, but the moment she sees the same invested with the dignity of type, she must needs exclaim against the impropriety! How in the world, then, are our manners to take healthier forms, if their abuses are to grow up unnoticed and unchecked?

Do not for a moment think, my dear Fritz, that my reception in the town has been such as to sour my temper, or to render my remarks the result of an embittered and unworthy envy. There is not a city in the world where a stranger is welcomed with more hospitality, and where his short-comings are treated with a more lenient hand; nor is there another upon this side the Atlantic, where a man can pursue the bent of his own inclinations, so little subject to remark and observation. Nowhere are the ladies more kind and conciliating; nowhere are the men more obliging and courteous. But in a new and growing society, where the old elements are all the while blending into new combinations, and where arbitrary distinctions are growing up to stand in place of the fixed but factitious ones of the European world, it is but natural that abuses should creep into the body social, and the gangrene of fashionable extravagance fester here and there in the system. God forbid, that in applying the caustic to the diseased parts, I should be ignorant or insensible of the healthful and vigorous action of what is sound and perfect!

But while I deeply regret the reproval of some, I am proud of that so freely bestowed by others. I did have a fear, that in proposing a series of observations upon the fashionable life of the town, I should in some measure seem to sympathize with that class of persons who rail ignorantly and blindly at whatever savors of wealth and respectability, and who derive their spiritual nutriment from such papers as the Sunday Courier. But by their most welcome abuse, they have convinced me of my error, and have relieved me of one of the worst embarrassments which beset me. I cannot enough thank such for their labor, and shall try hard to merit a continuance of their censure; only regretting that their capacities are unequal to the task of rendering it as pointed and forcible as would be wished.

WAYS OF GETTING INTO SOCIETY.

Cy n'entrez pas mâchefains praticiens,
Clers, basauchiens, mangeurs du populaire,
Officiaux, scribes, et pharisiens,
Juges anciens, qui les bons parroiciens
Ainsi que chiens mettez au capulaire.—GARGANTUA.
Liv. I. Cap. LIV.

Tophanes, who is something of a philosopher in his way, as well as a wag, has arranged from his note-book, what he calls a schedule of the prerequisites to fashionable success. He has arranged it in the pretentious manner of those public economists and politicians who make a reputation by their synopses and arrangement of figures. It certainly has a business-like and authentic air; and though I must confess to ignorance of its entire credibility, as well as to sundry of its allusions, it shall come in precisely as he has prepared it. Prerequisites:—

1st. { Money, Name, Swagger.

2d. { Person, Impudence, Mr. Browne.

3d. { Display, Music, A Coach.

4th. { Parties, Politics, Invention.

5th. { Literature, Moustache, Taste.

6th. { Religion, Propriety Honesty.

7th. { Good-Nature, Modesty, Indifference.

Following out his analytical arrangement, Tophanes has written against each item of his schedule the names of such as have gained, or still maintain position, by possession of the prerequisite with which they stand credited. But since I have taken Heaven to witness, in the name of old Le Sage, that I have no personal intent, the names must be suppressed.

But although these are noted as the prerequisites, they are not always the absolute causes of success; and I am assured that not a few with unbounded means, either from lack of name, or too great impudence—or, what amounts to the same, too great modesty—are reckoned quite upon the outskirts of society. Others again, with abundance of swagger, yet from a want of either money or music, are in an almost hopeless state of exile. Still others, possessing creditable names, are so unfortunately addicted to propriety or religion, as to render them utter outcasts. Even Literature, as Tophanes informs me, without the aid of a moustache, or Mr. Browne (who I suppose to be a writer for the Literary World), is a mere nullity; and many a poor poetaster, in sheer ignorance of Derby and Martell, has uttered lamentable Jeremiads over his fallen state, and hung his harp upon the willows. Religion of itself is not altogether hopeless, provided it be of a striking and brilliant sort—well spiced up with startling doctrines, which are altogether in advance of the old hum-drum order. Thus, a bishop who has a leaning toward the worship of the Virgin, or a layman who is strictly tractarian, or a lady who inclines to private confession and rosaries, or a trinitarian who verges upon the unity, or a papist who curses the Pope, are all in a fair way to make their profession brilliant.

Taste will do very well, but must be properly guided ; and I am assured, that several interesting, and well-intentioned young men have ruined their prospects by too great independence in this matter. It is by no means worth while to express an opinion about a new opera, or a new picture, before ascertaining the views entertained by the Home Journal, De Trobriand's Revue, or the Courier and Enquirer ; and if these could be confirmed by the opinion of a 'distinguished leader of the ton,' the sooner they are promulgated the better for a man's reputation. As for expressing a contrary opinion, none venture upon it, except a few stupid *fogees*, who frequent the Society Library, and who read the London Athenæum.

So with regard to etiquette, and the *parure* of balls ; nothing would be more fatal, Tophanes tells me, than for a simple-minded young man to advance observations upon these subjects, which would militate against those entertained by a 'French nobleman,' or Martell.

Taste, upon the whole, appears to be rather a dangerous element in the character of an aspirant; and if it be rude—that is to say, cultivated under such old-fashioned teachers as Burke, Alison, and Reynolds, it had much better be kept in abeyance, until it shall have become rounded into the graces of the town *dicta*. On some topics, indeed, a little latitude is allowable, such as Forti's singing, or Melville's last book, or Mrs. Butler's horseback riding; but woe be to the unfortunate young man, who in a moment of forgetfulness, should express admiration for Beneventano's voice, or smile at Sanquirico's pantomime, or think Truffi any thing but exquisite, even in black satin.

Indeed, it would be quite unsafe for an ambitious young man to venture without some previous preparation on the score of tasty remark, into one of our town galleries; for if he should inadvertently linger before a painting which had not received the stamp of approbation from those who guide in these matters, it would at once blast his reputation. I am not a little surprised that some of our publishers who have latterly taken to stealing occasional matter from the journals, should not venture upon the preparation of a little text-book of taste, carefully compiled from the Home Journal, the Day-Book, and Sun newspaper, with notes by the author of 'Etiquette,' and a preface by N. P. W. They might adorn the title with a Vignette—an Hyperion head; and for tail-piece, they might adopt a prize of the Art-Union.

You will be on your guard, then, my dear Fritz, when you come to the city; and don't make your friends blush by running counter to the town standards; get hold, if you can, of an odd number of the *Revue du Nouveau Monde*, and post yourself a page or two in taste.

> Και ταῦθ' ὁ χρη'ζων, λαμπρὸς ἔσθ', ὁ μη' θέλων
> Σιγᾶ'.

Whip up your Greek, Fritz, and tell me if this line from Euripides comes not as pit-pat as in the Attic Stage-piece, or as any on the fly-leaves of St. Leger? 'Follow the town umpires of taste, and you may achieve a reputation; neglect them, and you had better be dumb;' and this translation is as near the mark, as Gliddon's interpretation of the hieroglyphics; or as any Opera lady's construction of the *quel che fa*, in Don Giovanni.

As for music, it will work social wonders, absolutely Orphean; and a young lady who cannot boast her two or three months' tuition from some

Signor Birbone, is lost to all hope of success. Gentlemen who are without a decided bent in that way, should cultivate a certain intensity of expression, which is to be worn at all private concerts, but rarely to be assumed at the Opera : he should also learn the meaning of *barytone*, *soprano*, and *contralto*, and if possible pronounce them with the Italian accent ; he should occasionally look over Saroni's Musical Times, and get some crude notions about the difference between the German and Italian composers. It would be well for him to know something of the personal history of Lablache, or Grisi, and he should speak enthusiastically of Meyerbeer, and rather doubtingly of Duprez. If caught in the society of those who really talk knowingly on these topics, it would be best for him to keep silent, look very wise, and to fill up the intervals of talk, by humming the 'Last link is broken,' or Yankee Doodle.

It would never do to admire the old fashion ballad singing ; and as for psalm tunes, a man had better be caught listening to 'Love not,' from the band of the Anatomical Museum.

But I must defer, my dear Fritz, saying what might be said of town coaches and politics, in their connection with social position, to another letter ; and I shall entertain you, while your are smoking the lower end of your cigar, with a fragment of a *curious diary, from a fashionable friend of* Tophanes'. You will see that he is almost as little used to journal making, as many of our later writers of travels; but there are sparks in him of capital good taste; and, if I might use the language of the town critics, though not very scholar-like, it is clearly the production of a gentleman, and perhaps a soldier. Tophanes has recommended that it should be entitled the

DIARY OF A FASHION HUNTER.

Dec. 20. Went to Trimum's party last night; danced with Miss Thuggins,—rather tasty, but devilish blue. I wish she wouldn't wear such a ridiculous head-dress; found everybody laughing at us; very well for a chat, but musn't dance with her. Talked with Mrs. Knowem,—a good lady to be acquainted with, ugly as sin; but then she's a favorite, and good-natured as possible; offered to take me to the Blinkum's—kind of her. Hope it'll be stormy, so we can go in a carriage; don't like to be seen walking in the street with her. Must send her a bouquet.

Dec. —. Called to-day on the Blinkum's—rather cool; but had enough compliments ready to warm 'em down; must get a new stock against I go again.

Got an invitation to receptions—shall accept; shan't be very particular; they are nice people, very respectable, but confounded poor.

Dec. —. Go to a ball to-night at Widge's. They say it's a splendid affair; hardly know how I got an invitation. (*Mem.* To call on Browne to-morrow, and settle up; he'll be blabbing.) Want confoundedly to get an introduction to Miss Blank—capital dancer, and very distinguished-like; it would be quite a feather to take her up to supper; must contrive it somehow; mustn't forget to wear the embroidered waistcoat—that's killing. Am afraid I shall meet Mrs. Dandy, a dear good friend—do any thing for her; but she'll keep me in the corner for an hour; must try and not catch her eye. How infernally she does dress!

Jan. 1. Fagged out! Let me see—a hundred and fifty calls,—there's a gain of forty-two on last year—capital gain too—all top-knots! The Widge's rather cool, but then half a dozen saw me there—that'll count. There's a stupid set a body must call on, or they'll be talking him down, and that'll never do. After all, it's cheap to get a good word for a visit once a year. Mean to go in a carriage another year, if the salary don't fall off.

Jan. —. Got an introduction last night to Miss Tubins; she's an heiress—a hundred thousand, they say, in her own right. She's a little literary—wish I'd known it before; might have quoted any quantity from Byron and Shakspeare. (*Mem.* To look over book of extracts.) Is it best to call on her? Am going to the Opera to-night; hope she'll be there; no idea of being particular; but then it's a capital thing to be seen with an heiress; it makes people talk. And then again, chatting during the music is capital; it makes one appear indifferent, as if he had heard better in his day; and, moreover, it allows you to put your head very close to a lady's ear, which looks very familiar and confidential-like. It looks well. (*Mem.* To put some peppermints in my vest pocket.)

Jan. —. That cursed fellow B—— tells me he suggested my name to Mrs. Figgins as a nice, gentlemanly young man—first among the 'admissibles'—and yet haven't got an invitation. Must look very bold and unsuspicious when I pass her carriage; think I shall give her a downright stare. It'll look well—as if I had never heard of her before. Bowed to-day to the Miss Widges—think they took it kindly; must call some day next week, and rub up my French a little before going; they say they talk French capitally. Should like to manage to walk home from church with them some Sunday; all the world is out, and of course it will make remark. They say, too, they are great church women—better humor it. (*Mem.* To look over Dr. Hawks' tract on Auricular Confession, and to buy a new box of pomade.)

Jan. —. Wonder where Shanks buys his cravats? They have a devilish pretty tie. Ask Mrs. Beman about it, and when the new shirts are coming home. Am going to the Dangle's to-night—magnificent house, fine flowers, plenty of money, but only *so so* for 'blood.' They say she wants to 'work up;' think she may in the course of a winter or two, seeing that the ——'s have done as much. Wonder what it'll cost her? Shall try, I think, to get into their graces; they'll be grateful for attentions—know they will. Needn't be afraid of compliments—can put 'em on raw; they can't see the edges. They say Mrs. Dinks visits them, and she's of an old family; must find her out—meet her as if I knew her; it'll tell well.

Jan. —. Got an invitation to Swivel's;—made his money by some small manufacturing, either saddles, horse-shoes, or book-backs, but musn't decline. Besides, he has a pretty daughter, though she don't know much;—all the better for that. Am to dine out to-morrow. Wonder who'll be there? Must look over my dinner stories: heard a deuced

8

good one the other day, but afraid I've lost it. Wish I had learned to sing.

Met Stokoskinski the other day; wonder if it'll pay to ask him to dine? He's a vulgar toad, but then he's a lion: it won't do to lose him: and these poor scape-goats are, they say, very grateful for a dinner.

There's Mangle, too—has written a book,—I don't know what: strange that the ladies can regard such fal-de-ral matters; but they do. I must try and see him—of course, meet him as an old friend, and tell the women I'm intimate, and that he's a sad dog. The jackanapes won't know the difference—talk to him about his book, and I'll play him just where I want him; he's as poor as a crow. (*Mem.* To step into Putnam's, and ask what he wrote?)

Jan. —. They've got a new singer at the Opera—wonder what they say of her? Must call on Mrs. H——; it won't do to be precipitate; can't depend now on the Home Journal; they say it's growing fashionable to dispute even W——. How shall I manage to get at some of ——'s literary soirées? To be sure, they sneer at her, but it's sheer envy, besides, one sees the lions, and as they say, a great many first-rate people; and gets a deal of serviceable matter

—rather heavy, but do very well to spice with. Should like to know an artist or two; one gets supplied with genteel terms about the paintings; and that reminds me to buy an Italian Dictionary; what the d—l is *chiaro-scuro?* Miss Sweepstakes asked me the other day, and had to tell it was a particular sort of varnish; hope it is.

Jan. —. Went to a concert last night with the Swet's—horrid hot, and stupid. But then they are serviceable bodies, very respectable, and all that; very good recommends in case I want to get married; musn't let the acquaintance drop. What a fool I was to talk about the Opera—ought to have remembered that they were sad blues; must ask Wiley for a list of Dr. Cheever's works, and if not too long, commit to memory.—Asked the S——'s if they knew the author of Gringers, and pointed him out; it's all very well to know these characters, but it is bad to talk too admiringly,—best to be a little flippant, and patronizing. Shall try and get acquainted with Dr. G—— of the Prose Writers; they say he knows everybody, and everything, and tells the oddest stories.! A devilish fine acquisition. (*Mem.* To ask him if he knows Dr. Headley?) By Jove, I *must* write a book!—think the Harpers would publish if I'd pay for the printing, and advertising, and guaranty against loss by fire; and as for its moral, about which they say they are rather tidy, why I'd stick a verse from the Psalms in the title-page, and dedicate it to some D—D fellow, or other.

Passed an evening a day or two ago at the Shrimp's—very learned indeed; quite scientific-like—talk Greek, they say; yet there was a capital set—uncommon respectable. Must cultivate the sciences a little more; wonder what the subscription price is to Littel?

Jan. —. Have just found out who drives that magnificent equipage with the splendid harness cloth; shall try and get upon speaking terms; to be sure, they are stupid parvenus; but then it tells well to take off your hat to a showy equipage. The talk last night at Fidge's ran upon books, and I had the stupidity to run off in a string of praises upon W's book, that I picked up in the newspaper. Found out that the Fidge's felt scandalized at something he had written; of course they looked horror at me; *must* be more careful;—will try and fish up some abuse against I go there again.

Jan. —. Had a visit from Mapes, a country cousin; what on earth sent him to town; the fellow will be insisting on my showing him the lions, and he's most unconsciously gawky. Wonder if he's got the money to buy another hat—am afraid I shall have to lend it. Shall change my lodgings in the spring.

Went the other night to take supper at Dobson's—a very scholarly sort of a catch, who wants to be a high liver, and all that; but he can't make it go,—at least, don't think so. Latin quotations won't go down now-a-days. He had better take to music or horses. However, it looks well to be seen with such book chaps—glad there are such—you get up a little reputation for book-knowledge, and as you don't use it, people think you are very modest;—I think so too.

Jan. —. It won't do, I am convinced of it, to go to a Presbyterian Church any more; it may answer when a man's established in the town, but it ain't fashionable: can't humor my religious scruples any more—feel attached to 'em, very much,—but it won't do:—must try and smuggle into Grace. The Holy Communion is very well, but rather low; besides, everybody can go there, so there's no particular merit. (*Mem.* To buy one of the fancy prayer-books, and get a velvet collar put on my coat.) There's more in this church matter than a body thinks for;—used to slight it, and go regular as a deacon to Dr. S——'s; but it don't *tell* at all.

8*

They say it's getting quite the thing to be vestryman; must lay an oar to windward for that berth. As for Puseyism, it's best to keep cool, and see how the wind lies.

Jan. —. Went to the Opera last night; got for a moment into the Shrimps's box—very chatty, but uncommon stupid: told the Blinkum's so, at which they laughed (never smiled at any thing I said before), and thought me very funny—asked me to spend the evening with them.

D—n it, I think I'm getting on!

Such, dear Fritz, is the rude but racy account which Tophanes' friend has given of his prospects and tactics. You will, I know, agree with me in saying, that it bears the stamp of earnestness, and very many internal proofs of authenticity. Very many of its allusions are of course unknown to me; but should they prove to be apt, and pointed, I shall insist on publishing further extracts. At the same time, I may add, that while Tophanes holds himself responsible for all the material statements of his friend, yet should any thing about them prove offensive to the parties alluded to, such parties shall have the amplest opportunity for denial or explanation, and their letters shall be treated with the utmost consideration.

CORRESPONDENCE.

We shall give the following letter and its answer; for although they are hardly worth printing, they may perhaps serve as an encouragement to such letter-writers as have never ventured out of the Sunday papers, or the Globe.

MR. TIMON:

Dear Sir,—I wish you would send me, soon as convenient, the card of your friend Tophanes. I think he must be a 'stick;' and I rather imagine he can give me the right sort of advice. For you must know that I've been hanging on the town nearly the whole winter, and yet the d—l of an invitation have I got.

Mind you, I don't act hurriedly in this matter. I want you to know that I've done all that a man could be reasonably expected to do. In the first place, I've paid Martell a bill of some $10 12½; I have cultivated what I consider one of the prettiest moustaches afloat; I have worn out nearly three dozen of Alexander's best kids at the Opera, concerts, at Grace Church, and on Broadway. I have even stepped into Crowen's several times to subscribe to De Trobriand's Revue—but confound it, I can't read French. I get my breeches cut at Derby's, and have sent a bouquet to Madame P——; besides, I've written a sonnet to one of the most fashionable ladies of the town, for the Day-Book (the Home Journal wouldn't print it), and sent her a copy.

My name is on the books at the New York Club, and I've got all the tittle-tattle of the day at my tongue's end; I don't wear a scratch, and as for the polka, I've been taking lessons all winter. It wouldn't be of so much importance, if these accomplishments had not given me rather a bad name down town; there's no hope of a law office, and my application the other day for a clerkship in a Broadway store was sneezed at. Couldn't Tophanes help me out?

Very confidentially

TIM. GREEN.

N. B.—They take in my letters at the New York Club.

P. S.—I forgot to tell you that I carry a cane, and part my hair behind.

REPLY.

Tophanes' compliments to Mr. Green, and would recommend to Mr. Green, Mr. Browne.

University Terrace, 5 P. M.

With this, my dear Fritz, I leave you to your quiet country avocations, until the mail of another week shall light up your solitude with a glowing No. V.

TIMON.

FEB. 21. NEW-YORK. NO. 5.

"Chi s'insegna ha un pazzo per maestro."—ITALIAN PROVERB.

THE Opera-going ladies are, of course, so familiar with Italian that I shall have no need to translate for them an Italian motto; but for you, Fritz, over whom ten years have rolled (and don't blush for your age) since you regaled yourself on stewed kidneys, and Orvietto wine, in the dirty *trattoria* that stands under the lea of the Roman Pantheon, I will render the proverb into plain English:—'Who teaches himself has a fool for his master!' And now for the application. Sundry wiseacres, guided by their own penetration, have fixed the authorship of these papers. Unfortunately however, both for themselves and the public, they do not at all agree in their conclusions; and my publisher has latterly supplied an inquisitive friend of mine with a list of no less than six or seven different persons, each one of whom had been represented to him as the undoubted author of the Lorgnette.

Among the names, I notice that of a prominent journalist, a classical editor, a newspaper reporter, a sagacious musical critic, a professed book-maker, a doctor of divinity, a vamper-up of old jokes, an erudite merchant, a slashing medical man, and—would you believe it?—an enterprising literary lady!

Indeed, I had the pleasure, at a late evening entertainment, of hearing the whole of the last number read aloud, from beginning to end. And it heightened not a little the mirth of the matter, to find that certain critiques upon the piece, which I hazarded in course of conversation, took vastly well, from their unsophisticated nature; and they even drew down upon me, in the end, the titter of the whole company, to think that a man should be so ignorant, as I seemed to be, of town society. To tell the truth, I showed such lamentable ignorance of the more pointed allusions, that the hostess was evidently much mortified, and would have come near to blushing—though she was over forty—had I not apologized, by pleading a recent return from the country.

The whole of this company, which was variously made up of keen, middle-aged women and astute young fellows of five-and-thirty, persisted in attributing the work to a certain gentleman of high scholastic attainment, who has spent many years abroad, and who was represented to me, as a person of extraordinary character in various ways. Of course, I expressed a great desire to see such a lion, and am promised, by my friend the old dowager lady, a sight of him at her rooms, on some evening of the coming week. She hinted, however, that I would do well to pay particular attention to my toilette on the evening of the presentation, since otherwise, he might serve me up in his next, as a bumpkin. I expressed due thanks, and shall appear in one of Wyman's best blue coats, elegantly set off with figured gilt buttons.

A young gentleman who was directly accused of concocting these weekly opinions in the book-shop of my publisher, met the charge, as I understand, with a simper, and a knowing smile—cocked his hat a little upon one side of his head, and attempted to whistle a stave from La Favorita, but broke up before he was half way through. These were certainly suspicious signs, and had their weight with the shop-boy.

The literary lady, too, as I am told, denied the

allegation with an air of evident embarrassment—as, indeed, any woman would naturally deny a progeny of so very equivocal origin. I wish to heaven, Fritz, that the state of our morals was such, that no lady of the town should manifest any greater anxiety to bely her offspring. And though John Timon blurts the matter himself,—if the town striplings did no more discredit to their parentage than the Lorgnette, there would be little need of sharpening up these 'studies of the town,' *aut res tangere acu!*

RESPECTABLES.

——— Vile bigots, hypocrites,
Externally-devoted apes, base snites,
Puffed up, wry-necked beasts, worse than the Huns
Or Ostrogoths, forerunners of baboons ;
—— dissembling varlets, seeming sancts,
—— beggars pretending wants,
Fat chuffcats, smell-feast knockers, doltish gulls.

GATE OF THELEME.

There are an almost incalculable number of *respectables* in town—both respectable things, as churches, eating-houses, slop-shops, and the like ; and respectable people, as lawyers, note-shavers, fops, and women. I have been puzzling my brain for a long time, in the hope of finding out what it was that made a particular broker or play-house respectable.

You shall have, Fritz, the result of my observations, though they are by no means definitive, and will serve only to show a few modifications of what the town, in its wisdom, is pleased to dub—respectable! Nor will I promise but that these observations themselves, shall be very much modified by further discoveries.

My neighbor, the grey-haired lodger above stairs, is certainly a most respectable man, though he has rarely a sixpence of change about him. He bears, so far as I know, a good name; is regular in his habits, and has struck me, notwithstanding a greasy coat collar, as the very pink of respectability —a sort of standard for the whole class of respectables. You can judge, then, of my surprise, at hearing my landlady say to a grocer's boy, who came with a heavy bill for spermaceti, lemons, and whiskey, against the tasteful lodger, and who was very urgent for the money—'that the gentleman would surely pay—that she had never had a more *respectable* gentleman in her house!'

But I find that it is not at all necessary to pay bills to be respectable; and have been credibly informed, that very many men about town—both authors and bankrupts—who are never known to pay bills, rank as highly respectable. Indeed, on asking the other day in regard to the character of a defaulting gentleman, I was assured that he was eminently respectable. My friend Tophanes informs me further, that certain ladies who are remarkable for very great eccentricities of dress, as well as certain obliquities of conduct, are notwithstanding, exceedingly respectable. An opera-singer was pointed out to me as being, off the stage, quite respectable; and a preacher, whom it was my fate to hear a few Sundays back, was represented to me as being, out of the pulpit, every way respectable.

A journalist who indulges in the most wanton caricatures of good sense and decency, is called a respectable man; and a publishing house, which supplies the slip-slop literature of the day, is represented as a most respectable house.

I hear in all quarters of respectable boot-makers, respectable dancers, respectable ladies, and sometimes, though more rarely, of respectable doctors, and even respectable authors; and I am only surprised that the Commissioners of the new code have not included respectability in their list of qualifications for jurors. So acute a man as Mr. F. should have had an eye to this matter.

In the general way, I find that a black coat a little threadbare is a very good type of respectability; but if it have a velvet collar, the matter is subject to doubt. A man who comes up from the country, and pays his house bill regularly, and who does not abuse the pavements, or the papers, may pass current as a respectable man for a long period of time. My landlady, I found, had recommended me to my laundress, as a respectable country gentleman, of respectable connections.

A respectable family, as I find, lives in a respectable, small house,—burns small fires, and enjoys the acquaintance of a great many respectable people. The master of the household does a small, but respectable business ; the wife dresses in very respectable dark *mousseline ;* the daughters attend a respectable school, and the sons are clerks in a respectable establishment. Respectable families are very apt to give tea-drinkings, where you will find a great many respectable old ladies, who sip Bohea out of blue and white china—who talk in subdued tones about the weather, the fashions, the scandal, the respectable books, and the babies,—and who discourage hilarity in the younger branches of the household, by saying,—'My dear, it is not respectable.' They have a small library of most respectable books, such as Pilgrim's Progress, Arthur's Tales, Science Made Easy, an odd volume of the Arabian Nights, and Headley's Sacred Mountains. They, of course, subscribe to so respectable a paper as the Commercial Advertiser. They have a most respectable way of talking, and do not say anything of anybody or any subject but what is respectable.

They have a respectable card-basket filled with very respectable names; and having passed many respectable evenings at respectable families, I can of course, commend them to you, Fritz, when you come up to town, as every way respectable.

The respectable lawyer (there are such) does a quiet, counsel business, dresses in prim style, and has copies of Chitty, Cowan, Johnson, and a thumb-worn 'Acts;'—he borrows the New Code, and Statutes at large, is Commissioner for Rhode Island or Ohio, has a respectable sign at his office door, and is known chiefly, if you are particular in your inquiries, as a respectable lawyer. If a bachelor, he dresses respectably (only respectably), lives at a respectable house,—will possibly, in time, unless a *ne exeat* be served, marry some respectable woman,—drink respectable sherry to his Sunday's dinner, and make out respectable 'writs of deliverance.'

The respectable doctor looks very grum at mention of the Scalpel, but subscribes to the Medico-Chirurgical—laughs good-humoredly at Forbes' wit—expresses respectable opinions of Brodie and Liston—owns a respectably bound copy of Velpeau's Surgery, which he never reads—does a respectable business—attends service at a respectable church (near the door, so that the congregation may suppose him to be absent)—wears a wise scowl—has one or two respectable criticisms in condemnation of homeopathy—drives a respectable gig—and is known as a respectable practitioner.

The respectable clergyman preaches respectable sermons, adapted chiefly to very respectable people; and he is, unfortunately, but too well satisfied with a respectable weekly attendance, and a respectable salary; his hearers are, of course, respectable; and he leads them at a respectable gait, toward the practice of a highly respectable Christianity.

A respectable author is of somewhat rarer accidence; it being generally understood among respectable people, that all the pith, wit, and point which go to make a writer popular, are by no means respectable. Dullness may be reckoned eminently respectable; and not a few of the town authors, with an eye to this last-named quality, have won a reputation for respectability, absolutely gigantic. Their works are read by all respectable old ladies, and are commended by the New York Express. But wo be to the writer, young or old, who thinks to tread on the prejudices of *respectable* society, whatever they may be! Wo be to him, if he thinks to enter any protest against the insipidities and hollow affectations of the town-life; or to plead with such strength as lies in his tongue or brain for a little more humanity of purpose—for a leveling of those hideous elevations which pride, or impudence, or gold, have built up in our most Republican City. Wo be to him, if he pricks, with a sting that punctures, the wind-blown reputations that conceit and effrontery have fecundated. Wo be to him, if his stylus, sharp as a knife, cuts deep into the calf-skin integuments that hold together our most worthy life of fashion. Wo be to him, if he attempt to lift off from the carcass of the body social, those flimsy, patched-up coverlets of respectability and propriety, which keep down the smell of its corruption!

Take breath, my dear Fritz, and we will come back to respectable young women. The term does not include genteel young women, or fashionable young women, nor yet play-actresses—unless, indeed, the united efforts of Mr. Maretzek and a prominent journalist, should snatch them from their fashionable perdition, and set them in fashionable salons. Irish servant maids are, of course, out of the question, and much more, those of American birth. French governesses and German teachers are always eminently respectable.

Respectable people are remarkably tenacious of their dignity; and they do not think it respectable for shabby-looking old ladies, in faded bombazine, to be shown into their pews at church; nor do they like to have young women in pea-green silks and ancient bonnets, ring at their door-bell. They do not like to have a poor, respectable man build on the same block where they are living; they do not think it respectable. They are cautious how they suffer their respectable boys to play at 'hide and go seek' with poor respectable boys. Of course, they give respectably to public charities, but do not like to ask their poor country cousins to dine with them, when they expect respectable company;—or to church with them, except on rainy Sundays.

We have seen, you know, Fritz, the best bred European ladies dining, and even chatting somewhat gaily with their *bonnes;* but it would quite shock the highly respectable women of our Republican town, to be seen publicly on any terms of familiarity with a dependant; it would not be respectable. It is even advisable to close the windows of a respectable coach, when the respectable owner is riding with her nurse.

Fashions of dress become respectable for respectable people, only after the milliners and fashionists have made them so. The Jagello hat, for instance, which we are looking for with intense interest, would be sneered at for a month by all respectable ladies; after which time of probation, it would become, by the ordinary current of the town-life, a most respectable hat; and all the respectable ladies would tie it to their very respectable chins. A stage play becomes now and then respectable; and the Serious Family, after stirring into mirth the critics and habitués, begins to draw a few *respectable* people, who steal in as it were, clandestinely, in respectable old hats; after a time, they come openly and laugh boldly at Burton, while between the acts, they assume a cool air of the highest respectability.

Ancestry too, comes in for a share of respectability, and is, I find, the source of a great supply of the staple. If fathers have not been altogether respectable, it is well for a respectable young man to go back to his grandfather, who, if he turns out one of the small fry of honest mechanics, had best be docked off the ancestral list, and a trumpery story dished up, of old English, or Dutch names, and connections. And such story will serve as admirable fecund matter for the ingenuity of those small artists who draw genealogical trees, and for those enterprising foremen of coach painters, and card engravers, who contrive coats-of-arms.

It should be remarked, however, that in adopting this course, the parties will overleap the range of respectables, and swoop down among genteel people, or even among 'leaders of the ton.' Indeed, for a matron of rather weak wits, who wishes to put her boys on an elevated plane—at the very top, indeed, of the parabola which Mr. W. has so gracefully cut out of an apple with his pen—it is much safer to be genteel, than respectable.

Respectability is, after all, slightly vulgar, and will not cramp inquiry or gossip, one half so well as decided gentility. Moreover, gentility, from the fact that it is a trifle more exclusive, comes less in contact with strong, investigating habits of mind, which might, in times of forgetfulness, prove fatal. A substantial coach, with the blinds drawn, and a magnificent house, very quiet, gloomy, and close, are almost impenetrable; and if the house should be opened for a ball, why the men are accessible (unless engaged on church business) who will supply music, suppers, crockery, carriages, and company, for a respectable commission on the valuation.

In the rub and jam, nothing will be easier than to escape irksome *tête-à-tête;* and the little *bijouterie*, and *papier maché* ornaments, will establish reputation on the score of taste—to say nothing of a few well-scattered French novels—De Trobriand's Revue, and a well-thumbed LORGNETTE.

Respectable tea-parties, you must observe, are subject to quicker scrutiny; they should by no means be indulged in, by those who have any doubts on the score of their breeding. You may take this as an axiom not without its worth :—vulgar people had better not ape respectability; it is safer to be genteel. Or, if I were to put it in the form of a syllogism—which, if it were not better than the best of Senator Foote's, I should be ashamed to repeat even to myself—it would be thus :—

Respectability promotes inquiry;

Ill-bred people are sensitive to inquiry;

Therefore, ill-bred people had best eschew respectability.

Please to lodge that middle term, Fritz, in your cranium, as another axiom which will prove explanatory of a great deal of town talk, and action.

As for Ancestry, I must say no more of it, since I am intending to furnish, with the aid of the gray-haired lodger, a full chapter upon pedigree; which, when it appears, you may be assured, will be as well worth possession by town livers, as the British Herd-Book to Durham-Cattle Breeders, or the Turf Register to cockney sportsmen.

Town respectability may be summed up, as a sort of emasculated honesty. It is a kind of decent drapery, which society purloins from what Burke calls, 'the wardrobe of the moral imagination,' to cover the shivering defects of poor human nature.

If you can say nothing good of your friend, at least, —call him respectable. If your neighbor has defrauded the business community, time and again, and yet lives in the best of style, prospering in a new commerce of coffee or cotton,—call him respectable. If a lady has forgotten herself, her duty, or her husband, she can creep under this elastic screen of respectability. If a clergyman preaches doubtful sermons, or practices doubtful sins,—dub him respectable. If you are caught chatting familiarly with your coachman, or your tailor, you have only to say—they are respectable. If your newspaper is dull and prosy, and given to long, tedious twaddle,—it is, at least, highly respectable. There is no vitality, no earnestness, and no independence in town respectability. There are plenty of respectable politicians, respectable writers, and respectable women; but I never heard of a respectable hero, a respectable Christian, or a respectable philanthropist.

OLD BEAUX.

"He has an excellent faculty of bemoaning the people, and spits with a very good grace. He will not draw his handkercher out of his place, nor blow his nose, without discretion."—Bishop Earle.

I now and then meet, dear Fritz, with some old vestiges of the beau-craft, which existed twenty years ago. They were nearly my contemporaries, it is true, but they have much the advantage of me in having kept up an acquaintance with the *beau monde* of the town, while I have been wandering, —Heaven knows where. They are quite curious specimens of our kind, and are deserving of one of those accurate observations, which my lorgnette is sure to furnish.

With no great physical attractions, they yet dress in the top style ;—perhaps sport a beard, or imperial, or both, to conceal the lines which age has wrought in their chins. They use the best pomades on the town, and are capital authorities for whoever is on the look-out for a good tailor, boot-maker, or barber. They sneer, of course, at what they call the frippery of the day, and are particular in their attentions to very young ladies. They are usually club-men, and assume a sort of dignity and importance in the reading-room and restaurant, which is graciously accorded them. They play a good hand of whist, at a quarter the corner, with some old-fashioned observances in the game, which would not have done discredit to Mrs. Battle. They take, too, a quiet pleasure in an occasional half hour at 'old sledge.'

They make excellent diners-out, and are sure to fish up an invitation or two a week, from some of their former companions, who have now homes of their own. They take the liberty of cracking very bold jokes with their friends' wives; and are partial to 'old particular' Madeira. They, of course, are full of anecdotes, more especially of that equivocal sort, which follows the retirement of the ladies, and which, for one hearing, are quite passable. They are full of wise saws about government and society; and are exceedingly violent in their ridicule of the parvenus of the day. Though they are not partial to parties,—most of them having become slightly rheumatic,—they pay evening calls, and are particularly earnest in their movements among the boxes at the Opera House.

They are great admirers of beauty,—make frequent mention of the favors they have received from certain ladies, 'they would not like to name,' and are particularly delighted when they are accused in private conversation, of being 'dangerous dogs.' They talk of marriage as if every lady of the town was on the *qui vive* to possess them, and as if they had still fair prospects of a numerous and stalwart progeny. They are great favorites at tea-parties, where spinsters congregate, and can handle a pair of sugar-tongs as daintily as their own legs. They are dabsters at a compliment; and some few of a literary turn, have been known on special occasions to make sonnets, scarce inferior to those of Mr. Benjamin. They have no charity for the small fry of authorlings, which swarm upon the town; and abuse them all in round style.

They know, of course, nearly all the world, and sneer very confidently at the few whom they do not know. They talk in a familiar strain with clergymen and editors of popular journals; and they cultivate a certain indifference and carelessness of manner in the bar-rooms, and in the street, which is quite remarkable. Nothing disturbs them more than to fall in with a really earnest man, who is disposed by his talk to prick them out of their lethargic state, and to try the metal of their old coin of opinion; they have no means of dealing with such a fellow, but to condemn him as a flippant coxcomb. They affect an uncommon knowledge of French, and of all the finer accomplishments; they are quick to detect, what they reckon breaches of etiquette, and are precise—even to pocketing a dry crust at table, to clean their white gloves for an evening.

They manage to get an introduction to most of the reigning belles, and talk much about them, though they know very little. They call themselves connoisseurs in brandy and paintings; and have a peculiarly sweet tooth for French *entremets;* and such as have an unpronounceable name, they think very fine. They wear a heavy signet ring, and cultivate a delectable familiarity with house-maids, and opera-singers. They assume a very patronizing way with the daughters of their old friends,—call them by their first names,—will sometimes venture a kiss,—write them valentines, and give them small presents of *bijouterie*.

They pride themselves hugely on a handsome foot, a genteel figure, or a very bushy beard; and express plaintive regrets for the great number of young women whom they have unsuspectingly made unhappy. They are fond of showing their friends little billets, directed in a very delicate hand-writing, and though they do not exhibit their contents, they wink in a way that makes one sympathize deeply with the unfortunate victims of their address, and agreeable qualities. They have a carefully cultivated laugh, and if their teeth remain sound, it is open-mouthed. They are of course very jocular and gay-humored, and are careful to conceal their occasional sighs; they do not like to read very fine print. They write very delicate notes of acceptance to evening entertainments and dinner parties, and seal with a very large private seal. They commit to memory the best portions of the musical critiques in the newspapers, and yet sneer at the critics as poor starveling vagabonds; they adopt the editorials of the Journal of Commerce on matters of trade, and yet turn up their noses at the opinions of the press.

As for profession, they are very likely (living on a snug two thousand a year) above that sort of thing; or perhaps, are plethoric bill-brokers, or silent partners in a jobbing concern, or small lawyers with a great many trusteeships in their hands, or doctors who visit respectable old dowagers, that have been lingering under hypochondriasis for an indefinite period of time.

And one of these very old beaux will read the Lorgnette over his cigar at the Club-house—his remainder bottle of port at his side,—his head inclining back,—his varnished boots upon a chair, and with the most self-satisfied air in the world will condemn the writer to perdition as an arrant literary coxcomb;—never once imagining that John Timon is perhaps his senior by half a score, that he has helped him out of innumerable scrapes, and has very possibly seen as much of the world about us, as he or any of his fraternity.

Pray take it kindly, old fellow; don't let your asthma or weakness in the joints annoy you too much; *semel senescimus omnes.*

There are old belles, too, my dear Fritz, who are biding their time; and when the humor is upon me, you shall have their portraits, even to the color of their eyes, and of their stockings.

—

CORRESPONDENCE.

I shall publish without any prefatory remarks, the following letter from a lady: if I might, however, be permitted to judge from a certain gracefulness of expression, and an indescribable under-lying of the *savoir-faire*, I should say that it came, not only from the hands of an accomplished lady, but from one who is perfectly familiar with the improprieties of the town.

My Dear Mr. Timon:

It has been hinted to me that you are an old friend of my former husband; if you are, I wish you would do me the favor to call; any little remembrances of the dear, good man are most satisfying. I want to tell you, too, how much I approve your work; your judicious remarks upon taste, I cannot praise high enough. I have long felt the want of just such a book as you propose. As for the polka, you've said just what you ought to say; it's a positive shame, the way our young folks do go on in these matters! Only to think that my little cousin Polly went so far the other evening as to lay her head outright on a gentleman's shoulder, out of sheer exhaustion ; why, Sir, it made all the blood boil in my body !

I've talked with my clergyman about it, a dear, good man, (are you a clergyman?) who makes long parochial calls. He says it's 'an abomination,' and he quoted a passage from scripture, but I have forgotten it.

I wish you'd say something about the way some people hold up their clothes at the street-crossings ; its growing worse and worse ; and I see they are beginning to trim off their drawers with delicate lace edgings,—as if such things were expected to be looked at, except by the chaste eyes of servant maids, and little poodles.

Do go on, Mr. Timon—you seem to me to be a sober, rational minded old gentleman ; and since my dear husband's death, I have met with very few of that sort.

Respectfully,

DOROTHEA.

P. S.—If you wish, I can give you my address.

—

Another letter which has come to hand, as my paper is going to press, appears to be from a vivacious young lady, of quick parts. She writes:

DEAR MR. TIMON:

I wish you would let me know who you are:—do; I think I could give you some capital hints; you know a lady knows a great deal that a gentleman never can know, try as hard as he may. Besides, I should like amazingly to dance a polka with you; I know from the way you write about it, that you must understand it a great deal better than the fussy little fellows who almost pull me over, and havn't got an idea of the spirit of the thing. A lady wants some sort of support,—doesn't she? I think you could give it, and not be pushing one about against the wall-flowers, and getting dizzy and stupid.

I and my cousin go to nearly all the balls; and though there won't be any but Presbyterian ones, now that Lent has come in, still I know some real gay blues, who dance as mad as any Episcopalians. I'll introduce you, and we'll have some capital times.

I've got an aunt, who says *such* witty things! Do let me know who you are. I'm not a bit afraid to send you my address; wont you call in the morning? There are a half dozen fellows from the New York Club, that come in every evening. I want to tell you something about them; they do say such stupid things!

Do you visit Madame T——? Try to. It's a delightful place;—such splendid oyster suppers! I don't care if you print this; only if you do, punctuate it, and correct the spelling. I'm so familiar with French, that I misspell my English half the time. Don't talk hard about the Home Journal; it's a love of a paper! I've written a letter for it that's going to be published by-and-by.

Yours, affectionately,

LUCIA.

—

I am most sorry to be compelled to withdraw my claim to Lucia's acquaintance. I am sure she must be a love of a girl; but Tophanes is her man, and I shall hand over to him the necessary documents. Nothing makes me regret my age and baldness so much as these little kind testimonials, from genteel young women. Still, Fritz, we can be young on paper;—and so, thank God, I will be young! and my pen shall dance its weekly fandango, as lively as the liveliest of the polka striplings, —though the rheumatics are warping my shoulder-blades, and age is wintering my beard with gray.

TIMON.

FEB. 28. NEW-YORK. NO. 6.

Ne demandez pas de quelle complexion il est, mais quelles sont ses complexions; ni de quelle humeur, mais combien il a de sortes d'humeurs. Ne vous trompez-vous point?—*La Bruyère.*

PARDON me, Fritz, if over your shoulder, and by a few taps upon the tympanum of your most friendly ear, I pass an explanatory word or two, for the digestion of our cormorant public. It would seem that I have been set down by not a few newspaper critics, gossiping ladies, and by some respectable book-sellers, (for whom I ought to say in way of apology, that they rarely read the books they sell,) as a caterer to the tastes of those who are facetiously termed by the Sunday Journals, and oyster-cellar men—'the upper Ten Thousand.' Now as I have no particular desire of being mobbed, or burned in effigy, and still less of being reckoned the pliant toady to any scale or degree of social eminence, I most respectfully decline the acknowledgment of any imputation of this kind. And although I by no means profess fraternization with those very earnest paragraphists who rail at the people 'above Bleecker,' as if they were altogether destitute of those human sympathies, which a kind Providence has mercifully vouchsafed to people in other parts of the town, (particularly Nassau Street, and Centre,)—and while I cannot avow an entire coincidence of opinion with the abettors of any Astor Place mob, or haters of Macready, or Forrest worshipers;—and though I do not feel at liberty to subscribe to all the pleasant inuendos which come from the lips of my neighbor the tasteful lodger, about the equipages sometimes seen in Leonard Street, and the coupès with closed windows, and the ball-room intrigues,—yet, Heaven forbid that Mr. Crowen, or any of his fashionable customers, from the subscribers to the Home Journal downward, should reckon me the mere caterer to the appetites of those only who are rich, or—even worse—those who would seem to be rich.

A rough-and-tumble observation of a great many phases of life, both in the Old World and the New, has taught me, that sincerity and worth are not confined to any particular station of society;—that modesty and purity are sometimes struggling under the motherly-imposed haberdashery of a belle; and that inordinate vanity, and a hankering after the lusts of the flesh, are occasionally tossing under the tawdriest ribbons that come from the Canal Street shops.

But poverty I find to be the same unfortunate bedfellow here, that it is in every quarter of the world —Monsieur Cabet's Icaria (which I have not yet had the good fortune to visit, save in the columns of the Tribune) alone excepted. Town poverty has at command but very indifferent means of concealing the vices which attach to it;—thus the poor buck from Greenwich Street, or the critical chair of the smaller newspapers, living on forty dollars a month, who swaggers upon Broadway of a Sunday afternoon with a poor cigar, and one glove, will be the mark for abundance of most friendly sneers from the Christian people who live along the way; and yet your pretentious man who pulls on his *couleur de paille* kids, upon the steps of the New York Club,—who sports a well-stitched palletot, and very square-brimmed hat,—who scents Julien's dinners, or the bouquet of mock Chambertin, as fondly, and yet as ignorantly, as his compeer does the Ann Street stews, or Albany beer, will not only escape the odium of condemnation, but will be counted a miracle of a man, by hosts of young ladies at the front parlor windows ;—not that the ladies are looking out ; on the contrary, they are very intent upon their reading, or with kissing the baby, and of course *very* unconscious that any such gentleman, in stitched palletot, is any where to be seen.

Now what the distinction is between these two, in purpose, dignity, or humanity—that one should be the object of adulation, and the other of sneers—I think it would puzzle a nicer inquirer than Mr. Calhoun to determine. Even in the matter of taste, which in a highly adulterated state, is the pabulum on which those disposed to fashionable display inordinately feed—the advantage may lie largely on the side of the Greenwich aspirant; and this, notwithstanding his rival of the Club shall have consulted incontinently the plates of *La Belle Assemblée*.

So, too, a rich Cashmere, and Miss Lawson's toggery of wadding, wreaths, and lacings, will not only make a crooked form straight, a blanched forehead ruddy, and restore fullness to the withered hulk of six-and-thirty, but they will marvelously deaden searching inquiry, and blunt the eyesight of popular sagacity. A poor girl who scrimps the frugal meal of a mother, that she may gratify her woman's vanity with a flimsy mantilla, or a faded hat ribbon, is smiled sourly upon as a worthless, heartless creature; yet the ladies of ton, squandering thousands upon equipage and laces, deaf to the low cries of a hundred mothers, going supperless each night to their straw pallets,—are elegant fashionables,—most generous lady patronesses of the Opera,—most worthy pew-holders,—most commendable Christians!

If, then, my observation should seem to confine itself to that class of society whose position ought to render it independent in action, and unimpeachable in character, it is not surely in view of making personal interest, for access to our Almack's, or to tickle a vanity which needs no delicate touches of a quill feather to be enlivened; or even were it otherwise, enough of the town litterateurs are engaged in the pursuit already; and I will do them the credit of saying, that their adroitness is only less commendable than their successes.

The LORGNETTE adapts itself, then, to what the booksellers may call, if they please, the higher circles, only because the lower ones have less need of the exposition intended. The follies of the latter are bald and palpable, while those of higher life need closer examination,—nay, they would at first sight pass for real beauties; but the lorgnette, properly directed, will expose—what touches of carmine,—what dust of pearl powder,—what shaven foreheads,—what ugly wig seams! How many follies need only a gilding to vanish; how many vices need only the covering of luxury to disappear!

When, therefore, Mr. Crowen, or my worthy publisher, think fit to announce to their customers, that the LORGNETTE confines itself to glimpses in high life, let them be fairly understood; let it be fully known that it is from no lack of earnest Republican intent, and from no desire to foster the prejudices of a self-constituted, prurient town aristocracy. In the honesty of a straightforward, country purpose, John Timon begs leave, not insolently, nor ill-naturedly, but firmly, and good-humoredly, to lay his pen upon such social sinnings of the hour, as seem to him worth the ink-lines of demarkation; and in the full knowledge, intuitively gained, and dearly cherished, that very many of those whose wealth and position are pre-eminent, will thank a stranger for speaking plainly of foibles, which they acknowledge, discard, and deplore.

And now, Fritz, having laid the matter straight between our obliging booksellers and the public, let us come back to our *moutons*.

LIONS.

—— "Veniunt spectentur ut ipsæ."—Ovid.

Lions, my dear Fritz, are not confined to the *Jardin des Plantes*, to the Regent's Park, to Welch's Circus, or to Timbuctoo. They are bred, it appears, in our town, and of such marvelous thrift are they upon the diet, which this climate and pasturage affords, that they will roar you, 'as 'twere a nightingale,' or as stoutly as any Joiner of the Night's Dream. We have, too, our allotment of dear good Mrs. Leo Hunters, who are on the search for the little cublings as soon as they are born; and if so be they can roar, though only so much 'as a sucking dove,' they will be fondled and nursed more daintily by them, than ever the sinning Ephesians by the old three-breasted Diana.

These zoologic patronesses are not only mighty quick of ear, but they have also a most delicate sense of smell; and they will scent you a young lion by the mere perfume of his mane, though his voice is capable of only the most incipient roar. They will feed him on such dainty food, and so tickle him in the throat and haunches, that presently he will roar, 'as would do a man's heart good to hear.' Thenceforth, he will be a caged animal, with his hours for feed, and his hours for relaxation, and be as regularly stirred up for the admiration of curious spectators, as the old Bengal Tiger at the Surrey Gardens.

These lions are not only highly useful in offering subjects for zoologic study to the common people, and in affording agreeable diversion to children, but they are of signal service, and I think I may add, highly profitable, to their zealous and sagacious captors. The methods of capture are numerous, and adapted to the size, strength, and habits of the animal. A well-roasted haunch of venison is considered very capital bait for full-grown lions, whereas whip syllabubs, and even water-ices, are used with great success, as decoys for the younger animals. Some few well-known lion-takers are so sagacious in laying their bait, that a strange lion can scarce venture within the town, but he is at once taken in their toils.

It is almost needless to say, after so much has been written upon the subject by Buffon and others, that the lion is the king of beasts; but I may safely add, what has escaped the notice of nearly all the writers upon Natural History, that the lion is a fashionable animal.

Indeed, there is scarce a lady of 'parts' in the town, who maintains an elevated position,—who is, in fact, a 'leader of the ton,' but has her bevy of lions, of different degrees of age, virility, and tameness. Some of these are so gentle that they can be safely led about, even in public places, without danger to the bystanders. Others are reserved for the salon—or, as I should say, keeping up the zoologic illusion—for the cages,—having a large run, but under cover. Here they are made to roar, by being fed or tickled. Others again are never dealt with, but on special occasions, being irascible in their nature, and at times somewhat dangerous. They roar only as the humor takes them, and have been known to show their teeth even to their captors. They are, however, somewhat rare; but are in great demand, and much sought after by connoisseurs. Lions, of course, differ in breed; some being of the royal stock—true Afric; and others of so diminutive a make, that those who are knowing in the matter, hint at the probability of there having been sometime a cross with the jackal.

The greater part of the town-lions are brought into the world under favor of the professional services of the gossiping journals; the Express newspaper is specially to be commended in this matter, and its delicate manœuvring would scarce do discredit to the best *Sage-femme* of the quarter of St. Antoine.

When fairly born, they are handed over to a standard corps of wet-nurses in the shape of penny-a-liners, and Mrs. Leo Hunters, who feed them on pap and such like dainties, as I have already stated, until they gain their full strength. Too strong food at an early stage is hazardous, and in some instances has produced a constriction that has carried off the young lions in a stage of tender infancy. Great numbers, too, of such as have enjoyed the over-nursing of the Home Journal, and the Literary World, have died from sheer surfeit; and yet others, who have been fondled in the arms of the old gossiping Lady, late of Broadway and now of Wall Street, have lingered only a short feverish existence—attributable, no doubt, to the crude and weakly nature of the pap.

Lions, as I have already told you, are of numerous sorts;—there are the musical lions, the literary lions, the critical lions, the political lions, the fashionable lions, the conversational lions, the playhouse lions, and the lions extraordinary.

Tophanes, who (I may as well say it) has been in his day a fashionable lion, has supplied me with a little epitome of their successive stages of growth; and I shall select from it such examples as seem suited to my purpose, at the same time adding largely from my own observation.

The musical lion, for instance, he tells me, if intended for public exhibition, must have a rhythmical foreign name, and be announced in the journals as the distinguished performer, who has repeatedly delighted all the members of the first European Courts, (I pray your particular attention, Fritz, to that word Courts, which has an uncommonly happy odor for all the lion hunters of the town.)

He must next have a private trial in a public room, possibly of the Astor, or Irving,—having previously invited the critics, who are spare, hungry dogs, to dine with him. This exhibition is heralded next day as one eminently successful, and as having given unfeigned satisfaction to a distinguished circle of unprejudiced gentlemen and ladies, of the highest critical taste.

The critics are honored with season tickets; the journals, (such as do the advertising,) are profuse of praises, and the Mrs. Leo Hunters are wide awake to secure a capture. He becomes a lion in the papers, is applauded at the concerts, is invited to a *soirée* at the house of a 'leader of the ton,' and repays the condescension of the *élite*, with a song, or a dexterous dab at his fiddle.

He has only now to manifest a proper *insouciance*, wear white gloves, and tolerably clean linen, to remain for his month the musical lion. Or if he fails in circles strictly fashionable, he can cut off his beard, and try his hand in moderate Presbyterian, or Baptist circles, where by cool, and assiduous attention, and naïve repetition of fashionable scandal, he may have a fair chance of renewing his age of heroism.

The private musical lion gains his degree without any newspaper noise. He is talked of in very extravagant style by the young lady who sings duetts with him; he volunteers (by request) his aid at an amateur concert; and if he be really deserving in voice, or execution, or possess any special attractions, or even pleasant eccentricities, he will be pounced upon by some watchful old lady hunter, who is needful of just such advantageous commodity to give a 'pleasing variety to her receptions.' He is petted, invited earnestly to come and pass an evening—sometimes (but more rarely) asked to dine—is talked of—wearies his lungs with constant effort,—is entreated to favor that charming young lady with the love *chanson*,—is assured that his voice is absolutely bewitching,—is urged to sing a duett with the lady in pink,—can of course make no refusal to the deaf old lady, who has been shedding tears—would 'exceedingly gratify a distinguished amateur' by repeating that passage from the Puritani—in short, he finds himself unsuspectingly, become the property of the lion-hunting town.

As for Jenny Lind,—whose name has been, I do not doubt, bobbing in the reader's thought ever since he commenced the reading of this musical topic,—there is no estimating the height to which the Lind fever will run, by the time of her landing on this island. Already the shirt-makers are advertising Jenny Lind Kirtles, and we shall soon have Jenny Lind ties, stomachers, and cuffs. Blue eyes and light hair are more than ever rejoiced in; we shall have before the summer is over a whole army of Jenny Lind babies; and the nurses will take good care to pinch the noses of the young bawlers into the Jenny Lind shape.

As for the gentlemen, Mr. Barnum will be able to double his Tom Thumb fortune, by selling them scraps of Jenny's old shoes for love charms; and if Mr. B. is properly grateful for this suggestion, I shall expect a generous *heel-tap* from him, on my own score.

Fashionable lions are to be found in plenty: they are those you will read of, Fritz, in your fashionable weekly, as 'leaders of the ton,' 'distinguished patrons of the Opera,' eminent foreigners, or French or Italian noblemen. They are of course cordially hated by all shabby genteel people, and are treated with marked indifference at the hands of such as, by sensible conduct, and independent action, are placed beyond the need of any lion favors. These lions, however, are in great demand, and have been the making of a great many unfortunate belles, and witless coxcombs. They are not supposed to be engaged in any other pursuit, than simple study of the *savoir-faire*, or what amounts to much the same thing, the *far niente*. If, however, they lend their faculties to verse, music, or painting, it is understood to be only in the form of accomplishment—an accomplishment which, however doubtful in its merit, will be sure to bring down a great clatter of golden, and most disinterested praises from all whose position is uncertain.

If housekeepers, these lions live in fashionable streets, and keep fashionable hours. They will not be guilty of any such stupidity as allowing an Irish servant maid to attend the door-bell: they will insist on reception-days,—first, because it gives opportunity to shine in their own sphere, before numerous admirers; and next, because they may be sure of having their chair in the best possible light—the stupid books all out of sight, the little poodle in a clean ribbon, and their man Fidkins in his best white gloves;—and there will be no possible chance of their being mortified by the stupid Irish nurse rushing down stairs, with the baby in her arms, to see who is calling—simply because on that day the key is turned upon the nursery door.

Their topics are fashionable topics: the Hague street matter is commented on in a sad, sad way, very much as fashionable clergymen talk of the destitute heathen of Polynesia. They never walk Broadway at unfashionable hours; and the color of their equipage will give the cue to a large portion of the equipage-driving town. A hint in the Paris correspondence of the *Courrier*, as translated by an eminent Journalist, will lead to the selling of their bays, and the spanning together of black and gray. A marriage will be negotiated in the best Paris style; and it will be announced by an amiable penny-a-liner, who has been kindly smuggled into their punch-room, on a reception-day, as a high-life marriage, in which the beauty and grace of the young bride was only equaled by the elegance, and fashionable contour of the distinguished and fortunate bridegroom.

It should be said, however, in justice to the class, that no lions are more innocent than fashionable lions; they are not ill-tempered, or savage; they are the most good-natured lions that can possibly be imagined; their roar would never 'frighten the Duchess.'

As much, however, cannot be said of the critical lion; he is a useful attaché to old ladies, to the editorial corps, and young authorlings. He sneers at mere literary lions, and boasts of having given them their rank; he is cheek by jowl with the publishers, and is perfectly *au courant* of all that is transpiring in the literary world.

He dashes out opinions upon pictures, statuary, and music, as freely as upon books;—pushes his name liberally into print, and wears an air of such recondite observation as astonishes and perplexes young authors and school-girls. He mixes his pills of praise with such chemical tact, that a little irritant will go down with the lump,—just enough to inflame the mucous membrane of the vanity, which lines the whole stomach of an author,—and so, keeps the poor dog mindful of the power and agency of the druggist.

He is of course familiarly acquainted with everybody who is worth knowing, and is on terms of intimacy with vast numbers of extraordinary men. He assumes an air of high dignity at small literary *soirées*, is very patronizing toward young authors who are beginning to be talked about, and will even condescend to dine with them (at their expense). He affects something of a foreign air, and may perhaps boast, though it be only through books, of foreign cultivation.

He is coy of commending American success, whether in music or letters, simply because his much boasted principles of taste are not inherent and sound; and because he trembles greatly lest their suggestions should carry him counter to the courtly charts of foreign importation. Thus while he professes himself a patron, he is in fact the worst enemy to true republican endeavor.

It is this, my dear Fritz, that I want most to stigmatize—this coy-stepping, fearful, England-worshiping spirit of American criticism. It is a base habit of measuring everything by the standards of the old world,—which may be great, indeed, but great only by their association with the old world fallacies. In taste, in ease, in grace, in a cultivated *idlesse*, and in all the appliances which go to make life an amusement, and not a peril and a work, I grant you, Messieurs critics, that the old world leads us, by very much; yet surely therein lies no reason for relaxing the effort to create in our social life, our literary opinions, and our more earnest action, an independence of things European. Are we not, under God, the administrators of a grand political, and even social experiment; and shall we not have pride enough to reckon successes by their agreement with the great principles of freedom and equality—of manly dignity, and individual earnestness,—rather than the factitious standards which belong to an older, and what we righteously deem a false system of polity? Let us not bow down to courts, though we have warmed our vanities in their blaze; and let us not bespeak courtly sanction, though it rise like sweet incense in our nostrils. When shall we cease to be provincial in our tastes and judgments, and begin to be American, and earnest?

But—*revenons à nos lions.*

The literary lion is of somewhat casual and accidental celebrity; a few, indeed, of large growth, are much in request, and will command, at all times, very full salons. The growth of the lesser ones is something curious in its way, and worthy to be set before you, Fritz.

The prospective lion must be supposed to have written a book, or perhaps to have edited a book, or if not this, at the very least,—to have written a preface for a book. He must bespeak early the friendly services of those sly old paragraphists who live in remote corners of the town, and who are employed for a 'reasonable' compensation, as supernuıneraries in the offices of the journals. He will expect this in most instances, by sending a copy of the new book to the old gentleman, 'with the kind regards of his unknown, and humble friend, the author.'

Upon this, spliced with a mug of punch and a cigar, the young lion may count upon a complimentary line or two, which his private friends, if properly advised, will be studious to promulgate in every possible way. A huge placard bearing the title of the book, and the name of the new author, will be hung in a prominent place at the shop doors. His literary friend whom he has invited to dine, and whom he has pushed into remarkable good humor, with a bottle of Heidsieck, writes a captivating little paragraph for a prominent journal,—naïvely wondering who this new and rising author can be, and intimating in a most delicate, and scarce perceptible way, that he has a brilliant career of prosperity, and heroism fairly dawned upon him.

The Mrs. Leo Hunters are now fairly put upon the scent, and address rose-colored notes to distinguished editors, asking the pleasure of their company, and begging that they will introduce to them the new author who has been so highly commended. The new author has now only 'to help himself,' and without further effort becomes enrolled upon the zoologic list. He is presented as the writer of that 'charming book,' and our lady patroness has a prettily-contrived compliment in store for the gentleman who has 'beguiled so sweetly her hours of ennui!'

The lion, at this early stage, should not forget how to blush; indeed, it would be well to—positively blush,—bow,—be very glad,—be very sorry it is no better,—regret that it was carelessly written,—express boldly the opinion that it was not intended for publication,—disclaim the distinction of authorship, &c., &c.

At all which the lady patroness will rally him with very tender and approving smiles; and introduces him successively to Mrs. Mulkins, who is a charming old lady, of extraordinary literary taste; to Miss Bidkins, a poetess of very great grace; to a green-spectacled old gentleman, who looks very astute, and says very cutting things, in order to inspire the young lion with a proper degree of awe;—to a distinguished foreigner, who is *bien charmé* to make the acquaintance of the author of—(he forgets—*ne se souvient pas de nom*, for which he asks a thousand pardons);—to a lovely little girl, who looks languishingly at our author's moustache, if he has one, or his eyebrow, if he is without; and lastly to a decayed spinster or two, who express themselves very extravagantly in admiration of his work, and go on to quote some lines from Lord Byron, which of course the young author is very familiar with.

The lions of a month or two longer standing, will meet him with a little hauteur, which by degrees will wear off into an eminently patronizing manner. Miss Sibdilkins will beg the honor of his company on a certain evening, that she may introduce him to an eligible young lady, who has been in raptures with his book.

Corner conversations of very young ladies will centre very naturally on the new lion; and though I can hardly hope to throw the grace of their lively *bon mots* into my serious page, yet, Fritz, you shall be tempted with an echo.

"Isn't he handsome?" says one.

"Not handsome, but then *so* intellectual! I wonder if he is married?"

"No, they say not."

"What a forehead!"

"—— Yes, and lip!"

"—— And such eyes!"

"—— And then his nose!"

"—— Yes, and his chin!"

"And such a dear moustache!"

"And what dear stories he tells about those African girls!"

"—— And those naked Islanders!"

"—— That sweet little Alice!"

"—— And those grisettes!"

"—— And those Spanish ladies!"

"How they must have been in love with him!"

"I shouldn't wonder; but do you know they say"—— (and she whispers something about dissipation—wild fellow—at which they put their handkerchiefs to their faces, and turn their eyes up to the ceiling.)

"Oh, I don't believe it," says one.

"Besides so far away," says another.

"I wish I knew him; will you introduce me?"

"Yes; but then—you know—that dear Strinkiski—you promised to present him."

On a moderate computation, Fritz, I am assured that the number of literary lions reaches five or six a season; after which period of zoologic eminence, the greater portion sink into comparative obscurity, and sustain a miserable and precarious existence between newspaper paragraphs and tailors' bills.

A most abominable feud exists, as I am told, among all classes of these lions, and I am credibly informed that there is not so much as a pair of them, who are not pawing, and roaring at each other. They seem to delight in pulling out each other's manes; and as for anything like literary amity, or cohesion, they are as far removed from it, as from an International Copyright, or from any really manly effort to better the condition of their craft.

Even now I have given you no sketch of the more prominent literary lions, and have not even touched upon the political and extraordinary specimens.

You see, my dear Fritz, how this labor of painting the Town-life is growing on my hands; and there is reason to fear that this soft dalliance of the Spring breezes will catch me half through my labors, and lure me to a share in your country companionship. Meantime give me your best wishes, and splice them with a mug of your mountain ale.

TIMON.

MARCH 7. NEW-YORK. NO. 7.

"In our day, the audience makes the poet, and the bookseller the author."—SHAFTESBURY.

"Geese were made to grow feathers, and farmers' wives to pluck them."—DR. SOUTHEY.

I HAVE a long letter in store for you, my country Fritz, upon the authors and authorlings of our day; but meantime, by way of prelude to that full orchestral overture, I want to tell you something of the booksellers' opinions.

The sentiment which I have taken from Shaftesbury contains a truth, which I had not believed to be so palpable, until I had become, in virtue of my present vagary, a sort of book-maker myself. This accident of position has brought to me a little knowledge of the craft of book-making, and book-selling, which is not without its value, and which may come in from time to time, to point a moral of my text. My anonymous character has render-ed this observation more truthful and easy ; for the shop-keepers have by no means thought it worth their while, to withhold, from motives of delicacy or interest, any information sought after by a plain country gentleman, who secures their good graces by a courteous admiration of their shelves, and oc-casional purchase of a shilling pamphlet.

I have entertained myself not unfrequently by long chats with my worthy publisher, who, as I hold all communication with him by writing, is quite ignorant of the identity of his gossiping cus-tomer, with the editor of his 'smart little weekly.' He of course speaks very highly of the merits of the Lorgnette ; affirms that it has created 'quite a sensation ;' insists (very properly) upon the high moral tone of both paper and author, and is quite confident that it will have its effect in improving the tone of the New York society. Like a shrewd man, he of course varies his tactics with the par-ties he has to serve ;—to a young lady, he dilates upon the piquancy of the sketches of high life which the paper contains, and piques her curiosity by pointing out, with a knowing wink, certain initials, and *blank* allusions, which he recommends to her especial attention.

To an old lady, he either talks of the serious and moral caste of the affair—as being a very proper matter to be placed in the hands of children—or he commends in vivid terms its stores of gossip and scandal. To an old gentleman of literary habits, he enlarges upon the finish of the style, and the clear and bold character of the type. To young gentlemen of a rakish appearance, he hints that they may find in it touches upon etiquette which will prove diverting. To critics, he commends his paper as fair game, contenting himself with the moderate praise—that it is 'worth their reading.'

He further amuses one by the sincere and manly air with which he denies all knowledge of the author; and on my remarking casually, that I was a stranger in the town, he commended the work particularly to my notice, as giving a very fair and just view of the town-life and habits; and he begged leave to say to me further, that he had no doubt, for his own part, that it was the production of a man of considerable mark in the literary world,—and that all the statements to the contrary in the paper itself, he was compelled to look upon as 'sheer gammon.' I evinced my agreement with his opinion, and my gratitude for his compliment, by buying an entire set, and by entering my name for all the future numbers, which he told me with an air of authority, would amount to at least twenty.

Another bookseller thought the chief objection to the work was its size ; twenty pages of matter, now-a-days, is so mere a trifle in the book-world, that it is not easy to find a man who is willing to undertake the reading of so small a quantity—much less at the cost of a shilling. He thought if the author could be induced to increase the matter by half, and reduce the price to sixpence, it might prove a profitable thing—to the publishers. As to the author's additional labor, he seemed to regard it, as most publishers do, very much like so much vapor, or wind (I fling you here, Fritz, the handle for a witticism, at my cost), which was only to be thought of, in connection with the capacity of the cylinder, or vessel, which the kindness of the publisher was to furnish for containing it.

He compared the LORGNETTE, in this view, with one of the flashy novels of some two hundred pages, at two and sixpence ; and with an enormous weekly, containing, as he said, fourfold the matter, for the small sum of six cents.

Another bookseller, of large experience in his line,

thought the paper altogether too quiet for the spirit of the day. 'If,' said he, 'these sketches had been written in the style of 'Napoleon and his Marshals,' or Mr. Poe's works, or even of the 'Monk's Revenge,' they would have been in great demand. The public taste wants, just now, high spicing—a great deal of ginger and mustard; and if the writer had ventured to be a little more severe, and made personal attacks, or even given personal descriptions like those in the elegant summer correspondence of the Express newspaper, with dashes thrown in for vowels, there would have been no possible doubt of his success.'

Another thing, he very kindly told me, which went much against my letters, was the evidently unbefriended state of the author. 'He doesn't seem,' he told me, 'to have secured the good offices of a single journal, or to have a good-natured paragraph-writer in the whole town clique;—of course he can hardly hope for any puffs. Depend upon it, sir, these little puffs are the making of books now-a-days, as much as advertisements are the making of pills, or 'bosom-friends' the making of women. The publisher might mend the matter somewhat, if he would enclose a curt little notice to several of the journals, with a long advertisement, or a small bank note—but that is his concern. Moreover, a literary adventurer, as this fellow appears to be, is fair game for the whole tribe of critics to peck at, and no editor thinks it worth his while to say a good word for a person that nobody knows. Good opinions are not so cheap now-a-days, as to be hazarded without an equivalent, either in money or flattery.'

'If,' said a publisher whom I happened to have known in the country, 'this author, who seems to be a handy fellow with his pen, would make up a dashing book of travels in some new country, such as the Rocky Mountain Region, or along the Guatimala shores, I have no doubt but that it would meet with a fair sale, and I should not object under suitable guarantees, to undertake the work of publishing.' On my hinting that possibly the writer might not be familiar with those regions, he answered that it made but very little difference;—that in fact, one half of the more popular books of travel, just now, were made up by persons who had never visited the localities described,—that it was only necessary to make the general features and geography correct,—that, in short, the Universal Gazetteer and Morse's Cereographic Maps afforded sufficient data for a man of proper genius to make a reputation in that line. The old class of writers, who dealt stupidly in facts, he informed me, were now quite given up, and were not worth consideration.

Even the soberer subjects of History, he told me, must be re-vamped in some tasty way, and all the little tittle-tattle of the times, if it could only be seized hold of, would go farther to make a history-writer great, than all those leading political facts which used to be considered essential to the very name of history. And he instanced in this connection Mr. Parley, Mr. Abbott, and even Prof. Frost, who, by proper attention to this habit of the popular mind, had achieved immense reputation, and what was still more rare—indeed almost unknown with the whole race of American writers—very considerable incomes.

A popular publisher of startling pamphlets, has conveyed to me privately, the suggestion of putting my periodical into more popular shape, by introducing some extravagant *diablerie* upon the cover, printing in blue and crimson, and by giving more details of private life than I have yet ventured upon ; and he hinted that if it could be made up in the literary style of a late pamphlet, the 'Rich Men of New York,' with a little of scandal interspersed, in what he was pleased to term my 'very readable style,' it would be much more to my credit, and he would engage to take three hundred copies of each number off my publisher's hands.

Of course, my dear Fritz, I should be very ungrateful not to be anxious to please the booksellers, who are so full of their friendly suggestions, and who are so clearly anxious to please me. But as the gaining of a little money is not so much my object, as the gratification of a curious desire I am possessed of, to say whatever my humor disposes me to say—in my own way, at my own time, and at my own length—I shall hold on very pertinaciously to my present system, until my letters are done. Meantime, however, I would not object to proposals, coming from respectable publishers, with suitable references, for entering during the summer upon a two-volume book of travels in Ethiopia, or along the Upper Mississippi—a short, didactic homily upon the 'Rochester Knockings,'—'Unpublished Poems of John Milton, by his great-grandson,' or 'Astounding developments connected with the life of Q——n V-ct-r-a!'

Do not think, Fritz, that I am disposed to misjudge the bounty, or the literary acumen of most of our town-publishers. Not a more charitable body of men, in their way, than our publishers and booksellers, are to be found in the world; and the number of authors who are maintaining from day to day a subsistence upon their benevolence, is, I am told, past all computation.

It has even been suggested by the refined and elegant of our town (and the suggestion does even more credit to their heads, than to their hearts), that a committee of the most respected authors, with Dr. Griswold at their head, be named, to erect some suitable testimonial to a well-known publishing house of C—— Street;—to commemorate its Herculean and most self-denying efforts, in encouraging a taste for an elegant and refined literature; and in creating, by its unwonted and most praiseworthy attentions, an *esprit du corps* among American authors, which has given birth to a pure and a manly spirit in our indigenous literature.

A design, which would not be improperly committed to the genius of the distinguished architect of the late Bowling Green fountain,* might embrace a colossal statue of a prominent member of the house, with one hand clasping to his bosom the Wandering Jew, and James' last novel, and with the other raining down gold upon the Bryants and the Sedgewicks;—while at the watch-fob, in the

* This *chef-d'œuvre* consisted of a magnificent structure of native American rocks—arranged with an eye to the picturesque—over which the waters constantly bubbled, in most graceful and unceasing jets. It was found to leak badly, however, and has been taken down.

nature of a charm, might hang a copy of 'Harper's Pictorial Bible.'

An inscription might be written on the pedestal, rendered classical by Dr. Anthon, but spelt according to Webster in the vernacular :—

THIS HIGH MONUMENT

IS BILT BY THE GENIUS OF AMERICA, TO HONOR

The Most Distinguished Actor

ON THE THEATER OF AMERICAN LETTERS.

MUNDO MATER LIBRORUM FECUNDISSIMA,
NOBIS NUTRIX VERBORUM LIBERRIMA.

—

"Non possebat enim rumores ante salutem ;
Ergo postque magisque nunc gloria claret !"*

But not to a single house should all such honor be due ; generosity and literary kindliness are universal in the profession ; and dozens of impoverished publishers are understood to be the martyrs of books, whose authors are dining sumptuously every day. Is no new Horatius Flaccus to be found?

* A little latitude of translation, Fritz, is allowable in our day ; were it otherwise, I think I should not be very wide of the intent, that scholars would put upon the couplet, in rendering it by this doggerel :—

He didn't reckon honor so highly as his purse,
So now there's not a man, whose honor shines the worse !

Will not the author of 'Liberty's Triumph' make an ode in honor of our Mæcenases?

To this topic, my dear Fritz, we will recur at our leisure.

THE OPERA.

"Why, if thou never wast at court, thou never saw'st good manners; if thou never saw'st good manners, then thy manners must be wicked; and wickedness is sin, and sin is damnation."—TOUCHSTONE.

I have not as yet, Fritz, given you a look at what passes for the nucleus of much talk, many amiable newspaper quarrels, and very erudite criticism,—I mean the Opera. It was, I must admit, with a little pardonable vanity, and perhaps *finesse*, that I put upon my cover the name of 'Opera-goer;' knowing very well that without such passport to fashionable salons, scarce a single number of my paper would be sold. But since the suspicion, as I learn through my publisher, is now afloat, that John Timon is in fact no Opera-goer at all, and is only making pretences toward a fashionable distinction, which does not at all belong to him, I must do away with it at once, by placing you within the doors. And I may tell you, Fritz, that to be placed within those doors, either as critic, belle, or spectator, is a circumstance which would greatly help you out in any intentions you might have upon New York society.

To be an Opera-goer, is in fact a sort of distinction, which very few can afford to be without; and nothing but extraordinary distinction, a very reputable name, or superior attainments, can in any way balance a neglect of the Opera-house. There is a charm in the very name of Opera-goer, to all who are in search of eligible young men; and a seat secured by a bachelor, or a box of a regular subscriber, are *points d' appui* which nothing but the most gross inattention can fail to render efficacious, in securing a respectable position among those who guide us, in matters of taste, etiquette, and morals.

At the same time it is a distinction which must be coyly ventured on; and a little undue haste in posting one's self thus far, has sometimes subjected the unfortunate aspirant to most invidious abuse.

Thus a grocer, upon the eve of rising above his business, and making a stir with equipage, and balls, should by no means venture at once upon Opera-going: it is too hasty a step, and will induce remark about his knowledge, or appreciation of the music, that if he be at all sensitive, may provoke him to a retort, which would be social death;—or to a relinquishment of endeavor, which would, of course, forever debar his girls from an entrance upon the social platform. He should gain, by coy means, a little street position in the first place, and should endeavor to win *respectable* opinions by bounteous suppers, or by heavy subscriptions to popular charities—such as the Washington Monument, a Dickens ball, or contributions to political *roués* who make successful speeches; and after a winter or two of this management, well backed up by plenty of German music teachers, and a pew in Grace Church, he may safely venture on securing a pretty *loge*, and taking to it his daughters, three times a week, arrayed in the prettiest of Martel's beetle head-dresses.

A bachelor has the same observance to keep in mind; and without some such position as membership of the New York Club, or sometimes driving a tandem, or invitation to Mrs. J.'s parties, or at least a fair place on Mr. Browne's roll of 'admissibles' may give him, it would be quite unsafe to make the Opera-venture. He would inevitably be set down, either as a curious music-lover from the country, or some poor starveling of a critic, and not receive the notice of so much as a single opera-glass.

At the same time, it may be said generally that the subscription to an opera-box is a safe venture in its way, and will, under favorable circumstances, do more to establish a man's position upon the town, than any subscription for the building of a church, or the very largest of private, and quite ignoble charities.

Such absurd, and unnecessary acts of benevolence as endowing a school, or helping out of their straits a poor family, are of very little worth in comparison with a liberal opera support ; and they will really do no more to make a man's name respectably known with the leaders of our ton, than if he were to subscribe to the Church Record, or go to morning prayers in Lent.

I could easily draw my pen over the names of not a few unfortunate gentlemen, who, by a most incomprehensible devotion to such indifferent matters, and persistance in a quiet, and most unostentatious scale of charities, have forfeited all opportunity of securing for their wives and daughters, however attractive they may be, high social eminence, or even the most casual mention in the fashionable papers, or the billiard-room of the New York Club. Such men sin, too, with their eyes wide open ; and if they lose caste and social position, the loss will doubtless be rendered more harassing by the conviction that Mr. Maretzek, his troupe, and their newspaper admirers, have, with a generosity and foresightedness which do them honor, placed within their reach, at a small cost, every hope of achieving eminence.

Indeed, the Opera company, and above all, the managers, may be regarded as missionaries, who have, with a disinterestedness and love of souls, most commendable, left the attractions and luxuries of European Society, to come to this land of almost Pagan socialism ; and they are here putting forth their best efforts in a variety of ways, to save us from our lost condition, and to bring us nearer to the elevated plane of fashion, morals, liberality, and taste, which they have left behind them. They find too, fortunately, not a few, who are willing to take them by the hand, and cheer them in their undertaking—nay, to give them the aid of little piquant paragraphs of praise, which go forth like so many gospels of mercy, to redeem us from our social barbarism, and to gather us into the sheepfold of —— Opera-goers.

Were I disposed, Fritz, to the Carlyle manner, I might exclaim here—What heroism ! what devotion !

Music, and the love of it, high as they seem to stand, are, I assure you, but secondary matters, and entirely subordinate to that higher culture of what is elegant in chit-chat, and striking in address, for which the Italian missionary house offers such wonderful facilities. Where can a man find a more lavish display of the beauties with which Providence has adorned the faces and figures of *the* sex? where a more delectable interchange of pleasant and instructive conversation? where can a man gain easier an exalted position upon the social gradus? where can he put off better the air of his shop, and the taint of his shop-keeping ancestry? where will he have better opportunity of studying the anatomy, not only of the social life, but of *poitrinal* development and action? where else can a man look for patterns of moustache, head-dress, or gloves? where else, in short, can be found such a theatre for observing the successive advances of town-society, in taste, refinement, and all manner of polite accomplishment?

The boudoir, in the comparison, is but a green-room to the stage; the salon, but the field for little excursionary forays; the ball-room, a recreative play-ground; and the old-fashioned parlor-circle, but the arena for sensible stupidities and frightful proprieties.

Fritz, my dear fellow, when you come up to town, take a box at the Opera! You will gain position, refinement; and by assiduous attendance, you will acquire a cultivation that no mere book-reading can blunt; and a *bien-seance* that all the good sense in the world will be utterly unable to subdue.

If you are painting now upon the retina of your remembering eye, a vision of those great Italian Opera-houses, such as San Carlo, where tier above tier of eager ones, half shielded by the façade of their dimly-lighted *loges*, are listening to the music, or receiving their evening salutations,—let me beg you to mend the image. Our Opera-house is constructed more especially to see, and to be seen; such quiet hearing-place as a box of the fourth tier at La Scala, would pass without a call from American Opera-goers.

The Italian Opera had probably (as the biographers say) its origin in Italy; at least we have a right to infer it, from the language in which it is usually recited. It seems a natural exponent of the character and fancies of a poetic, passionate, musical, and idle people. You will remember, Fritz, our earnest admiration, years ago, of the *recitativo* of the street-singers in the long Via Toledo; and our listening by a midnight moon, in the city of Bologna, to the musical patrols;—scarce less enchanting to the imagination of a foreigner, than the leaning towers, the sausages, or the Guido pictures of that old city of gloomy arcades. It was but natural that the Northern cities of Europe should, for the gratification of their traveled and luxurious population, and above all, their courts, introduce the Southern music, and should secure, by their superior wealth, the first performers. Hence it is, that the Italian Opera finds its best presentment in Vienna, St. Petersburg, Paris, and London ; that is to say, the *primi* singers are superior in those cities, while the chorus maintains its excellence in the south.

With the importation of other foreign luxuries and habits to the American metropolis, the Opera could not fail to make its appearance. It commended itself singularly to those who had brought back from the Old World a love of its peculiarities and courtly tastes—saying nothing of the few who would regard it as a pleasant souvenir of musical intoxication. From its very artificial nature, it would serve as the germ for a new amusement, to such as had exhausted their merely natural inclinations ; its enjoyment, or pretended enjoyment, implied too, the possession of a cultivated and artificial taste, which would lift it above the level of ordinary and popular appreciation ; and this would specially commend it to many worthy democratic citizens, who are forever on the lookout for any pardonable means of rising above the common atmosphere, and for breathing an air whose rarefied state should give a pleasing delirium to their senses.

Wealth, too, which had tried all the vulgar means of manifestation in houses and plate, was anxious to seize on a new medium of representing itself in alliance with what was dignified as an art. Young ladies, not lacking attractions, and not having the *entrée* of the salons where they might shine, could at the Opera, find a common ground of display, with the most high-bred. Whole families could rise from obscurity upon the wings of subscription tickets; and pining street beauties enter upon a new life of head-dresses, of *negligés* hoods, and pink-lined cloaks. Middle-aged gentlemen, too, whose position was indefinable, from some unfortunate prejudice attaching to birth or employment, could now appear in ball costume, and daintiest of neck-ties, and do the faint execution of forty-year-old bucks upon the belles of the hour. Ill-matched ladies, moreover, condemned to the society of such rheumatic husbands as could not venture to balls or concerts, might now secure their private boxes, and be ogled and admired by whomever they wished.

It was, in fact, a charming device for measuring our refined, democratic society, by general observation. But as it was to become in some sort the nurse, or directress of social education, it was deemed advisable to drop the ballet which had uniformly belonged to the Opera in Europe ;—so that tender nerves should not be rudely shocked, and that the amusement might thus become as pure and wholesome, as it was natural and enjoyable. There were no provisions, however, in regard to low-necked dresses and strong lights ; the Homeric women, or 'high-bosomed,' being reckoned superior to the *ballatrice*, or long-legged.

At first, I am told, the Opera had its *locale* in a comparatively humble situation, where it was exposed to the inroads of common people, and where the ton of the hour were horrified by the presence of a great many ignorant country merchants, from the neighboring hotels,—men who very sensible and business-like in their way, had neither the requisite finish of dress, or the right mode of listening, to adorn such shrine of taste. This defect has been remedied by placing the Opera-house upon a more elevated footing; it is removed to a fashionable quarter, and a special regimen of dress (that of the Queen's Theatre, London) has been adopted; without which, it is now generally understood, that the finer Italian music can be but very faintly appreciated.

These means and appliances have made the town Opera a most noticeable matter. Three times a week, during the winter, its sofas, music, and light have brought together all that was supposed to be lovely, or learned in our town. There may be, indeed, good, common creatures for household purposes, or such women as would make most excellent mothers without the Opera doors; but they cannot aspire to that apex of our social pyramid, which can be scaled only through the agency of our most devoted patrons of Italian song.

I have amused myself often, Fritz, in running my glass over the interested faces which grace this temple of our social worship. Admirers and ardent lovers of the music, of course they all are; but their loves do, somehow, wonderfully vary. You might see in one box some little fair-faced girl, not too modest,—just having left behind her at her school,—*amare*, the Paradise Lost, and *Porquet's Tresor*,—blush into our town-world under the daintiest of head-dresses, and with the most naïve attention to the scenes and drapery. She can scarce manage that huge lorgnette; but its handling has been well practiced; her glove is a fit; and if she do not see plainly, she at least seems to see. Her mamma, with eager eye, cultivated by such optic study, calculates, with motherly discretion, the range of the various lenses that turn that way. She slyly pulls the dress of her daughter if the poor thing is disposed to break into raptures at the music, when Mrs. J—— is only smiling. She chides her, too, if neglectful or inattentive, when the signal has been given by one of Forti's die-away efforts, for enthusiastic applause.

Yonder you will see a fresh aspirant for social honors, in the best of Miss Lawson's 'fixings,' studying—not the scene, but the conduct of a pair of old stagers. She is laying up in her memory, from observation of every fold of a lace mantilla, from every swoop of the neck, and from every manœuvre with the glass, a set of rules which, on future nights, will stand her in great stead. Another, not familiar with the atmosphere, but too naïve to be studying dress or attitude, is very fearful lest she, in some way, offend against the practices of that august court. She scarce dares smile at Sanquirico, for she sees a sober expression on the face of the elegant lady of an adjoining box; and when she is near dying with admiration, she blushes to find that her companion is talking behind her fan with the gentleman of the long moustache. She wonders, indeed, overmuch what she ought to admire; she wishes heartily she knew; but for her life she cannot imagine what are the rules of the Opera taste.

An old gentleman, the father of a family, who is not an habitué, but who has come to have an eye upon what he terms his wife's vanities, will sadly mortify his family and family connections, by yawning in the corner of his box. In vain the distressed wife will pinch his elbows, or put on an indignant scowl; in vain the daughter will look appealingly, and murmur reproachfully, 'Why, papa!'—the poor man turns to the stage, trying hard to smile—to look serious—to admire, as he gets the cue from his wife's glances; and he casts a timid eye to the boxes to see if his *gaucherie* is observed. Yet he is patron of Italian music, and will furnish his wife with an heraldic panel to her carriage.

The travelled admirer who is of course very artistic in her admiration, will assume an easy carelessness,—be very indifferent when there is show of pathos,—play with her lorgnette at a stroke of humor, and whisper in a languishing way to her companion, when the singers have achieved their greatest triumph,—that it is only *comme ça*.

The old ladies who are looking out for new eminence in these capitally-contrived boxes,—now that their ball-age is utterly gone by,—and who know as much of Italian as of music, and as much of both, as Sancho Panza knew of temperance, or Faublas of chastity,—will study pretty disposition of colors, and shades, and make their old eyes blaze anew with the opera gas, and coquetry.

The critic who is treasuring in his brain particular Italian expressions, and who cons his copy to learn the orthography, will look wise as an owl,—sneer when the vulgar old gentleman yonder is patting his fat hands in clamorous applause, and will listen intently, and with an artist cock of the eye, to the more delicate execution—which to the mass of our earnest Opera-goers (and perhaps to the critic himself) is as much Greek, as the Lillibullero of my uncle Toby.

As for critical appreciation and remark, it resolves itself after a few nights, and the issue of a few Journal leaders, into an established set of opinions, which do not vary to the end. Thus Bertucca, who has Italianized a French name and a French habit of song, is the 'wooden Bertucca.' Beneventano, with a voice windy as a blacksmith's bellows, is the stout swaggerer, who makes love like a butcher, but whose stature fills up classically the scenes. Forti, with nice ear, and artistic appreciation, is a trifle Jewish,—yet with no Hebraic volume in his lungs;—not handsome enough to be admired, nor ugly enough to call out raptures from eccentric ladies. Truffi is the Divine—the goddess of the scenes, whose action is the worship of the critics, and whose singing will cause a delirium in the pit. As for Benedetti, his retirement has been honored with more sighs of regret, than ever followed the best missionary *exposé* of heathen Polynesia. John Rogers at the stake (in the primer) was nothing to the martyred Benedetti. The new Thaddeus of Warsaw!—for seasons to come, ditties will be pointed with his name,—recorded honors will gather round his memory, and lady-sighs will thicken over him.

These, our Italian Divinities, my dear Fritz, have been the centres of more active conversation, and the subjects of livelier debate in salon, at ball, and upon the street, than all the political heroes of the hour—not excepting the sick lion of the South, now mumbling like Dagon in his cave, over the bones of his victims.

Go where you will, if only the aspiring beauties of our town be present, and the Italian aperient shall open the lady-talk, and lovers paying their vows in operatic fragments, shall sigh,—*Non so, perchè non posso odiarti!*

It would be impossible, indeed, to compute the amount of influence in our town, flowing from that company of singers who enjoy the presidence of

Maretzek. All the clergy influences combined,—the anti-dramatic counterblasts of the Tabernacle,—the secessions of distinguished doctors,—the newspaper letters of a bishop,—the *pro tempore* harangues of the Head of the Pilgrims, and all the fish-bladders of the Ecclesiologists, are dust and chaff, compared with the prevailing *animus* that enlivens the body of our opera-worshippers! Victoria is scarce so much the subject of talk in the court circles of London, as are our heroes of the Astor-place among the 'leaders of our ton.'

Carlyle says our people have not contrived yet any great, new, social idea;—let him sweat us out of the mazes of his contorted words, a greater one than this very Musico-socio-operatic Idea, belonging to our town and ton; and if he can do it, I for one, Fritz, will link myself to the herd of his admirers,—who, though capital fellows, with their inverted optics, to reduce every existing system to apparent confusion, are yet, like their great demi-god, the weakest of weaklings, to devise any tangible, or practical method of Reform.

TIMON.

MARCH 14. | NEW-YORK. | NO. 8.

> "Il vaut miêux souffrir d'être au nombre des foux,
> Que du sage parti se voir seul contre tous."—MOLIERE.

IT is the mode for periodicals of credit and ability, to give from time to time upon their covers, the 'Opinions of the Press.' But from these opinions are generally carefully eliminated all such as count against the merit, or success of the publication. Now as I wish to be *à la mode*, Fritz, and am at the same time too thoroughly a foe to all sorts of quackery, to deceive the public by expurgated notices, I shall give you upon the cover of the present paper, a taste of the opinions of Journals:—thanking most cordially those who have done me the honor of commendation, and entertaining at the same time, a most respectful sympathy for those who have 'not seen the point.' My particular favor is due to the erudite editor of the Express, who has furnished me with a sarcophagus in his columns, and a pretty epitaph from his French reading; a more successful *undertaker* in all literary matters could hardly be wished for;—his types make a fitting entombment, and his comment a proper shroud.

PEOPLE IN SOCIETY.

"Cætera de genere hoc, adeo sunt multa, loquacem,
Delassare valent Fabium ——" HOR. i. Sat. 1. 16.

Others like these are left, enough to tire
A Timon's pen, or all the Scalpel's fire.

Our neighbors next door, some of whom I occasionally see in the back-court, hanging out a bit or two of mock Mechlin to dry, or a crushed petticoat to be blown into proper rotundity, are worthy people, of whom my landlady sometimes borrows a half a pound of tea, or a little 'spirits,' to tincture the sauce for the apple-dumpling. I had expected to meet them nearer by at one of our little parlor-soirées, which came off not long since. After being presented to a very showy girl in green silk, who sang in bewitching style, and to an old lady in bombazine, who had a good deal to say to me,—about genteel education, I ventured to ask after the neighbors. My landlady shook her head quite seriously, and told me that though they were very good sort of persons in their way, yet they were 'not in society.' This would not have been so curious, if I had not remembered that the tasteful lodger had remarked to me a few weeks back, with a very sober, and I thought, sympathizing air, that the landlady, though a very nice person, was 'not in society.'

The maid informs me that this tasteful lodger 'goes into society,' once or twice a week, on which occasions there is a prodigious stir in his chamber; the maid is running up and down stairs with hot water and 'fixings;' and the tasteful gentleman gives very loud orders from the hall, about his varnished boots, and the carriage. The Irish girl dresses his wife's hair, and does the lacing; after which she uniformly steps into the parlor to have the landlady's opinion, which is, of course, always highly enthusiastic.

I must say that I have long felt no little curiosity, to ascertain what sort of society the tasteful gentleman adorns with his presence: but not until recently have I been gratified. Finding that the old dowager with whom I take an occasional ride, was really possessed of a carriage with a small device upon the door-panel, he volunteered one evening last week, to introduce me 'in society.' I expressed myself charmed, and at the time appointed, was duly ready. He gave a running glance at my equipments, which seemed to him to be satisfactory. We were set down at the door of a small house, in what he said was a *very respectable* street; though he had previously admonished me that I must not look for any very great style, as the family, though uncommonly high, were just now rather under the weather.

I was therefore somewhat taken aback, to find, on entering, an uncommon glare of wax candles, a good many plaster statuettes, and some very showy colored engravings, which the tasteful gentleman informed me, by a whisper, were by 'crack artists.' The everlasting folding-doors, or, as the author of Alice elegantly terms them, the bivalves were thrown open, and disclosed the usual vista of carpet, book-case, and arm-chairs. The last Home Journal, an elegant book in *papier-maché* covers, and an embellished copy of Tupper's Philosophy were upon the centre-table, while a folded number of the Express was doing duty underneath a leaky flower-pot.

The lady of the mansion, upon my introduction, met me with a certain assured manner of the town, well calculated to astound and bewilder a modest country-gentleman who was making his first *entrée*. She asked me, with a glance over her company, if I had seen much of New York fashionable society ? and upon hearing my embarrassed denial, was clearly disposed to cheer me up, and to treat me with very much of that kind and pitying regard, with which missionaries look upon unmitigated Pagans, or as our voyaging tourists regard such Marquesans as are ignorant of the nature and uses of petticoats.

An elegant young lady in bare arms, three flounces, and massive gold bracelets was at the piano ; her head, set off with a wreath of green leaves and blackberry blossoms, was thrown a little to one side, and she was singing a fragment full of *cuori* and *amanti*, with delicate accompaniment, in what my hostess assured me was 'most captivating style.'

She presently rounded it off with a whirl of the fingers over the keys,—serving very much like those notes of exclamation, which young authors are very apt to put at the end of what they reckon their pretty periods. The tasteful gentleman patted his gloves together, and declared that it was 'quite charming.' The hostess kindly offered to present me to Miss Thuggins, who was just now rising from the piano-stool.

Miss Thuggins bowed graciously. I thought—'it had been a fine day.' She thought 'yesterday was, too.' I assented cordially, and thought 'it had been an uncommon mild winter.' She thought —'very mild,—the mildest she remembered; though she did not remember many.'

Of course she did not remember many—how should she? I thought 'it was most spring.' She thought it was 'nearly.' I thought 'from her charming performance she must be a lover of music?' She tossed her head prettily, and thought—'oh, *comme ça*.'

I thought—'she must go occasionally to the Opera.' She thought '*our* box was rarely empty;' and she asked me what I thought of Forti, and then what I thought of Bertucca, and then—of Beneventano, and then of Don Giovanni? And she interspersed the questioning with pretty little opinions which, Fritz, you will find condensed in the last number of the LORGNETTE, or sown broadcast through the winter's file of the Home Journal. Occasionally an Italian term or two were thrown in, which, if my memory does not misgive me, were not strictly of Roman pronunciation.

This topic, and the last ball at the Widges being

duly discussed, I diverted talk to the evening, and toward the tasteful gentleman, who I supposed 'was an old acquaintance.' 'Only slight;' she had met him she *believed*, but she did not think he was 'in society.' I directed attention to our hostess, and, as in duty bound, spoke highly of her taste and accomplishments. 'Oh yes,' said Miss Thuggins, 'she's very well; I sometimes run in here on the 'Off-nights;' she's a good body, though 'not much in society.' Indeed, since her return from abroad (there was a little interruption, and she repeated) —since her return from abroad, she felt little relish for most of New York Society. 'Ah! indeed,' said I, (it is well, Fritz, to counterfeit a little surprise at any such announcement; but not too much; you should have 'half suspected it from her manner',) 'and is society so superior abroad?'

'Vastly, sir; such breeding you see, (she unclasps a bracelet,) and the gentlemen are so polished—so agreeable—so ——' And she reclasps her bracelet, and looks across the room with an expression of most intense *ennui*.

I ventured to ask 'if foreign society was accessible?'

'Oh no; but then we had *letters*, (with an air of indifference and careless dignity.) It was nothing but dining out;—one day at the Clarendon with a party of friends, and then down at Greenwich to eat white-bait, and then with a merchant who has a *bijou* of a place out at Hamstead, and then at Carleton Terrace; and in Scotland we met Lord Somebody at an inn, and were so sociable together—a delightful man, I *think* I have his autograph.'

Judge, Fritz, of my humiliation in talking with a lady of such extensive parts! 'This Miss Thuggins,' thought I, 'must be a trump card; doubtless one of the shining ornaments of the town society; she has very likely learned the *schottisch;* she is an admirer of Truffi; she has passable command of French; she even limps in Italian; she probably has her carriage—perhaps a coachman with hat-band, and very likely a seat in Grace Church, or even a coat-of-arms on her card, or over her door.

I determined to risk the mention of her name to my old dowager friend on my next ride. 'Thuggins,' said she—'Thuggins, upon my word, I don't know her.'

'But, my dear madame, she is an extraordinary young lady; she has a box at the Opera; she dined at a Scotch inn with a Lord; she wears tremendous bracelets; she talks French; she is horribly *ennuyée* by New York Society.'

'These are good points—very,' said the old lady. 'Fidkins, (pulling the check-line,) whose drab coachman comes to the kitchen for you so often—the rich grocer's you spoke of?'

'Thuggins, marm.'

'Oh,' said madame, 'I know now—a nice girl, I have heard, in her way; a parvenu—she is not 'at all in society.' By the way, would you like to call with me at the Widges?'

'My dear madame,' said I, appealingly, 'I should like exceedingly to know what it is to be in 'society' in your town?'

'*Justement*—at the Widges, *mon cher Timon*, we shall be in society.'

To the Widges we went. Tophanes happened to be there, and came across the room to say to me, *sotto voce*, 'Eh, Timon, getting in here? A devilish good place (*piano*) to come for suppers, but vulgar after all; interlopers,—well posted in music matters,—drive a good 'turn-out,' but only half a year or so in standing; and as for Monsieur, (*pianissimo*,) he is a d——n scoundrel!' And he moved off to tell madame how charmingly she was looking, this bright spring weather.

If you expect me, Fritz, to tell you definitively, from such observations as these, what it is to be 'in society,' you are hugely mistaken. To be in society is after all only a relative state of being, and changes with your company, like the kaleidescopic colors in a man's hand. You may meet with warm receptions, most kindly attentions, gentle manners, winning address, and extreme cultivation, yet it may not be 'in society.' You may be startled with most lavish display of wealth, or the most gorgeous of velvet cloaks, yet perhaps 'not in society.'

Impudence may set a man in society, or it may throw him out. Goodness will never bring him in, and it is a shabby standard of faith if among the elect. Particular professions belong to 'people in society;' but they are in the general way, professions without practice. The broker is dependent on age, brain, marriage, or presumption. The cloth-man (nothing now of coats or tailors) is subject to the amount of cloths he may bargain for,—whether by piece or bale. The dentist is in a most doubtful place, hanging as it were, upon the lip of society. The doctor (if of Divinity) passes current like old coin which rings with a jingle, though the device, or date of stamp cannot be made out. The physician 'in society' takes very few fees, has few patients, (except his listeners,) is tidy, prim, buckish, and marriageable. The bankrupt gives good dinners, is shy of his creditors, and is a most excellent churchman. Authors and pastry-cooks are of a doubtful class, depending very much on the tastiness of their wares : a piquant sauce to a *paté*, or a pair of pants to a lady Alice, will be irresistible.

Mr. B—— you do not know, or care to know, though you have met him affectionately in 'society.' Miss C—— you do not know, though you have hugged her in the waltz, and felt her breath steaming on your cheek—it was only 'in society.' Madame is a dear, delightful old lady—but only 'in society.' Mr. D—— is a man in 'society ;' it is for him not only a state of being, but of action. He has the most taking chit-chat of the Journals at his tongue's end ; he has studied Count D'Orsay's etiquette to a fault ; he wears a cravat as wide as the wings of a turkey-cock before moulting time ; he cultivates his incipient moustache with the most assiduous handling; he compliments old ladies for their youthfulness, and young women for their beauty, and ugly ones for their sweet expression; he goes to dinners, and wins the champagne for his stories ; he goes to balls, and wins a waltz, a supper, and a headache for his pains.

'To be in society' is not to be at home ; it is not to be domestic—nor religious, except at church, or when talking with the clergyman's daughter. It is to say things you do not mean; to know people you do not respect; to bow to those you despise; to smile without intending it, and to live in mockery.

To 'be in society' is a most extraordinary position;—for a man, it is more than virtual death of action, energy, or of anything worthy of his manliness. For a woman, it is to ensure her trappings the widest talk, her failings the largest scandal, and her salons the greatest crowd. For a belle, it is to push her into the best market for the poorest bidders; it is to expose her ancle, her bust, her features, her accomplishments, and her worth (if she have any) to as 'damned an iteration' as any in Homer's verse!

Passons, my dear Fritz; we must not get heated in this warm spring-time.

Tophanes has furnished me, in furtherance of this humor, which has just now seized me, a few transcripts from the journal of a lady 'in society.' It will I know amuse you, although it is not altogether an artistic performance; at the same time it does high credit to the class in which it found its authorship. It is *naïve*, straight-forward, and clearly written, without any suspicion of its being one day laid before the public. To the present state of popular taste, I am sure that nothing could prove a higher commendation.

JOURNAL OF A LADY IN SOCIETY.

"A lady's morning work: we rise, make fine,
Sit for our picture, and 'tis time to dine."

J. Shirley.

Wednesday.—What a sweet man that Signor Birbone is. But then pshaw. only a teacher! I must dress particularly well to-night; am to meet Kawton they say—a love of a name; and one of the most fascinating men in society. Why don't Martel send home that crimson head-dress? It's so becoming, the J——s say; and I haven't worn it now these three evenings. I think my voice is good to-night. L—— has promised to urge me to sing; hope Strinski won't offer for the accompaniment; he is so anxious that everybody should admire his playing, that he never has done with his interludes.

Marie is getting careless about my hair; must give her the *porte monnaie* that Stiver gave me the other day, and if Figgins sends a bouquet to-day, will let her carry it to the Minerva. What a dull time this Lent. and black doesn't become me at all; I can't look solemn without giving that bad expression to my lip.

Thursday.—Well, what a time, to be sure! Kawton is fascinating, very. How prettily he paid that compliment about American women, so much prettier than Europeans—such complexions; and he looked very hard at my neck. (N. B. Must be more careful about the pearl powder; Ma said she saw it yesterday on my forehead.) And then he polks so sweetly; I never felt easier in all my life; I wonder if he *has* money? To be sure, Mathilde says he's a great toady, but then he's a club-man, and knows so many distinguished men, I hardly know if I baited him enough:—to be sure, I didn't ask him to call; but then I told him what a delightful street this was, and that Papa said he wouldn't live in any other—so delightful, too, to be on a corner; surely he must remember.

Positively, I will not dance any more with that odious Scratch. Papa says I must not treat him rudely; he is very rich; but he waltzes so horribly, and then————! As for marrying him, it's another matter; but I needn't hurry; twenty-five isn't very old; and I know I can catch the old fellow any time. He is quite desperate, I am sure of it. How I should like to stir up a quarrel between him and F——; how they would talk!

Saw Noddle; he talks everlastingly; very well, they say; but who wants to hear talk at a ball? Besides, he admires every pretty girl he sees—the puppy!

Monday.—Went yesterday to Grace with the

Fidges—a most delightful place ; hope Papa will take a seat there ; everybody listens so stupidly at Dr. Hawks'. I do wish Strinski wouldn't talk French to me in society ; it's so embarrassing ! besides, there's no knowing who may hear you, and you *may* make faults ; caught myself *tutoying* him the other evening, as if I had been talking to Marie ! how provoking ; if it had been S—— wouldn't have cared ; it might have set him on ; he is too modest.

Tuesday.—Was pale last night, but wore the crimson head-dress, and took a seat near the scarlet curtains. I must try and send to Paris for some more of those gaiter boots, they are so pretty. Marie has been trying to show me how to hold up my dress as the French women do ; it's difficult, but then it's worth a little study.

What a handsome German teacher Miss Muggs has got ! I wonder if I had not better learn German ? I'll tell Papa that Dr. T—— has recommended it ; besides, it's very well to sing snatches from the German Opera ; it gives an idea of cultivation. I wonder where Mrs. Fidge gets that delightful perfume, and then she never has too much ; must remember to let Marie smell me, before I go out another evening. Miss Quiz asked me the other day what had become of Snap, who used to be so attentive? Oh, I told her, we were capital friends, better than ever,—and looked very conscious; dare say she will think I've given him the mitten; I do hope she will, for she is just the person who will tell it all over town.

Thursday.—Walked up street the other day with ex-President ——. What a dear, good man! And then such a feather to be seen walking with him. The Hidges saw me, and looked daggers; the Simpkins bowed two or three times; how very friendly they are getting! I wonder if we *girls* couldn't get up a class in reading with Prof. ——; they say he is so agreeable; and then it gives a delightful chance to *practice;* one can ask such funny questions, and all so honest. He isn't married either, and if I could only get him desperate! for they say these literary characters do get desperate; and how delightful if he'd only propose, and then go off in a consumption. Heigho—how sleepy I am!

Friday.—I do wish that odious Miss Thingum wouldn't be so familiar in the street; people will begin to call us intimates, and I am sure she's over forty. She's very kind, certainly, but I don't like to invite her to my *soirées*, she is so matronizing

THE LADY IN SOCIETY.

and old maidish; I must send the carriage for her some rainy morning, and ask her if she won't come and pass the day.

Sister Belle is beginning to be admired; how strange, and she only sixteen!—must insist on her wearing plainer clothes; must tell mamma that the hat is altogether too gay for a person of her age.

Saturday.—Went to the Opera last night; Forti was quite divine; at least M—— said so, and it's safe to say it. Mr. D—— came to our box, and chatted for half an hour,—a horrid creature; strange that he can't learn how disagreeable he is, and not at all tonnish; yet they say he is very clever—quite an ornament at Miss L——s. It's very well though, upon the whole, to have a chat; it relieves the uniformity of one's face; besides, if any one asks me who it was, I can say,—oh, he says such clever things!

Saw Stroskinski in the Miggs' box; what a moustache he has got! Must ask them to present me; they say he is all the rage.

Tuesday.—Met the Miggs' at the party;—promised to introduce Stroskinski, but didn't, though they danced three sets with him. I suppose Mabel wants to keep him to herself;—I'll pay her, the minx!

Had to dance with that little puppy, Spindle;

couldn't refuse, because he is of good family, and amiable as a country girl. He hasn't got a leg bigger than a pipe-stem,—and such a beard! Mean to cut off a little fur from the cat, and send him for a valentine——"*mon chat, Monsieur, votre* chin."

How it helps a flirtation to drink a little champagne. Upon my word, I carried it off capitally last night. What little squeezes one can give a gentleman's hand; and then the polka after two or three glasses—upon my word, it is charming! I must get some of those brandy lozenges Miss Fidge told me of; she says, they go straight to one's head.

I must learn, too, some more of those tender French expressions from Marie; it's a sweet, pretty language; have begun to read Raphael the third time.

Wednesday.—How handsome Bidkins is; and rich too, they say, but *so* shy. Danced the polka with him last night; told him I adored it: but he put his arm about me as if he were handling a Vestal—yet I leaned on him *very* hard; how stupid some men are. I think he must be a Presbyterian. I told him I was engaged for the *next* waltz, and asked him if he liked waltzing. He said he did—'rather.' I can't hook him.

I do wish I knew those Fudges; they give such delightful parties; everybody talks about them;

must persuade papa to go to the same watering-place with them next summer ; then I think I can manage it, particularly if Pa takes his carriage ; I can get an introduction, and of course they won't object to make a convenience of our carriage. What a silly fellow Bunkum is. It's plain enough he wants to please me, but he don't know how ;—only to think of his praising the Squids ! To be sure they are good friends of mine ; but then they are pretty, very pretty. And then, too, the idea of disputing me about the pictures, and trying to set me right,—the coxcomb ! They say he has excellent taste ; for my part, I should like to see it.

Thursday.—Heigho—two bouquets ; one from little Fidge ; what is the boy thinking of ? I suppose he's heard them talk at the club of sending bouquets to belles ; however, he is rich, and when he grows up, will, I dare say, be good for something ;—must thank him kindly, and keep him in tow. Besides, he is very useful ; he never objects to escort one—puts on shawls, and picks up the pins that you drop, and will go back for your ball slippers—oh no, it would be very ungrateful to slight little Fidge !

As for the other bouquet, it has no card ; who can it be from ? There's the handsome music teacher, I wonder if he would dare ? Well, I will have it in my hand when he comes, and ask him if it isn't sweet—watch if his fingers tremble when he takes it: and then I'll pull out a little flower from it—a forget-me-not, if there is one—and put it in my bosom. (*Mem.* to wear the open morning dress, with lace.) The poor fellow, he'll hardly have strength to get through his lesson! What if he should make love to me upon the strength of it; —how delightful!

I am not sure whether it is best to be confirmed; Dr. H—— urges me; but Miss Hicks, who is in the best society, tells me not to be in a hurry. So far as church attendance and devotion go, it's very well; it offers good contrast to one's action at a ball, and you get the good opinion of a great many proper ladies of excellent families; but then on Ash Wednesday, or any time in Lent, it may be very inconvenient; mean to consult the Squids about it.

At any rate, I must buy a book of sermons to have on a side table—get them bound up with a little cross on the outside. I wonder if Dr. Griswold hasn't written any good ones?

—

I am sure, Fritz, you will have been delighted with this fragmentary journal; isn't it naïve and earnest? Indeed, if I had any suspicion of who was the author, I would address her a complimentary note, and insist upon being favored with further extracts ; and if she will have the kindness to address her card, or any further communication, to John Timon, at Mr. Kernot's bookstore, she would confer a special favor.

I have already freely offered the use of my paper to such persons as might feel aggrieved by any imagined personal allusions ; and it is in virtue of this offer that I give place to a feeling letter, which seems to have been drawn up by the counsel of the person whose character has been unfortunately impugned. It is needless to say, that in alluding to Mr. Browne, (of whose name I had no knowledge except through my friend Tophanes,) I was utterly unconscious of doing injustice to a meritorious and useful member of society. Far be it from me to wound the feelings or to harm the business of any individual whose merits are so striking and timely as those set forth in the letter below :—least of all, an individual whose connection with the church should screen him from hasty or injudicious remark. My sense of propriety, as well as what is due to the Holy Catholic Church, would forbid.

Tophanes thinks from the style of the letter, that it may have been drafted by a distinguished member of the bar, Mr. B——y.

MR. TIMON :

Sir,—In some of your papers you have made flippant, and I think I may say, indelicate allusions to a Mr. Browne. A gentleman bearing that name, though differently spelled, has called my attention to the fact, and has consulted me (an advocate and attorney at law) upon the propriety of instituting an action for damages.

Believing, sir, that you are not insensible to the principles of duty and generosity, when well set forth, I have determined to address to you this letter of explanation and enunciation, which (if published) will set Mr. B.'s character in the right light; and by its publication (as mentioned above), the said Mr. B. will consider himself reinstated in the brilliant position which, from allusions made (as above stated), he had reason to fear might be temporarily (so to speak) obscured.

Mr. Browne, sir, is a man who perhaps has done more to the advancement of society toward its present elevated position than any other man, or indeed than any man whatever. Mr. B. not only possesses, by virtue of his ecclesiastical connection, a high moral consideration, but he is also the generous patron of very many young gentlemen who, without Mr. B.'s services, would be simply and purely—young men

Mr. B.'s fees are moreover reasonable ; he has never over-charged, even though supplying ladies with gentlemen of the first water; his arrangements are ordered in the most *researcha* style ; he gives advice in regard to the capacity of ball-rooms, the time of arrival, the disposition of candles, servants, fiddlers, and hackney cabs, which few men are capable of doing in an equally creditable manner. Moreover, he receives with proper decorum unattended ladies, sees to their safe delivery—from their carriage—and closes the door upon them discreetly, when the affair is over. He furnishes statistics in regard to character if desired, and can inform uninformed ladies in regard to pretensions, expectations, dancing properties, drinking disposition, gastronomics, and temper, of most of the young men in society.

Few indeed could be so poorly spared from the *beau-monde ;* and his retirement from his station would leave a gap that certainly no man of ordinary capacity could fill up. In that event, sir, which your injudicious allusions acting on a sensitive and deserving conscience might possibly induce, the ladies of our fashionable world would be at a loss to fill up their lists, the young gentlemen be without a patron, the carriages would stray about like lost sheep, the servants be wayward and fitful in their movements, and the whole charm of our social assemblages be gone. In short, without Mr. Browne, the balls would be without their ornaments, and the streets without a whistle.

Picture to yourself, sir, a man in an overcoat, standing on the door-steps, braving the storms of winter and the sleet of driving clouds, hour after hour,—calling out to the hackmen ever and anon, like a watchman of old,—deprived of the opportunity, even if he had the disposition, to go to the corner, for a drink,—watching over the horses and carriages of hundreds of dancing and immortal creatures,—and, sir, I think you will say that it is difficult for the mind to conceive of a higher and worthier philanthropy.

I have addressed you this in justice to my client, and if it be published I shall consider the honor of my client satisfied; otherwise, sir, the law must take its course. Respectfully,

ATTORNEY.

As I may have some testy correspondents in future, who may use threats to get their letters published, I beg to say that I have associated with me Tophanes as a literary assistant. I shall therefore have at command the same means of getting out of scrapes that is now so generally adopted by the city journals;—that is to say, in case any article may offend a pugnacious party, I shall have only to state 'that the responsible editor was absent,—that he deeply deplores the insertion of the offensive paragraph,—that he has known the offended party from boyhood, &c.

To be sure, Fritz, I have a dislike of imitating the contemporary journals in any matter; and it is only in view of getting out of scrapes that might endanger my incognito, that I should ever presume to take advantage of a popular chicane, which, to tell the truth, is as unworthy the dignity of a journal, as it is bemeaning to the character of a man.

My publisher advises me that inquiries are numerous as to the probable length of this series of Studies of the Town, and he asks what answer shall be given.

Tell them, Mr. Kernot, that when my whim changes, or the town reforms, the paper will be stopped. And this is as safe and credible an announcement as any in the Literary World, or the archives of the Historical Society; and the flash weeklies may whip it into their chit-chat syllabub, if they can.

TIMON.

MARCH 28. NEW-YORK. NO. 9.

"J'ai parlé beaucoup de moi dans cet ouvrage, sans recourir au pluriel. On ne peut me soupçonner de vanité. Je ne me nomme point: et en parlant de moi, on ne sait pas de qui je parle."

It is a capital amusement for me, my dear Fritz, to listen to the world of critical remark, which our unpretending correspondence calls forth. But I observe that like most criticism of the day, it is not so much based upon anything intrinsic, as upon the supposed capabilities and the reputation of its accredited author. I know no finer test, indeed, of the critical acumen of our literary anatomists, than the submission to their hands of some such amorphous and anonymous matter as these very papers.

Putting all their keenness to the work, they fancy they see some man's idiosyncrasy 'sticking out' in every line, and the whole is docked off with some popular cant of judgment, which has attached by habit to the supposed writer's manner. It is thus that I am running the gauntlet of a hundred opinions, and while I have been honored with the praise that attaches to a popular author, I find at times my mirth vinegared with the stinging condemnation that has swept some other unfortunate book-maker to literary perdition.

One kind friend has assured me that he was ready to produce irrefragable evidence, founded on parallel passages, to prove that the LORGNETTE was written by the author of a late popular romance. I argued the point at length with him, suggesting that the resemblance might have been accidental or intentional, but without avail. He prided himself particularly on his acuteness in those matters. Nothing, I find, is harder, than to convince a critic against his will. When he finds that he has done me so gratuitous honor, my only hope is, that he will not, as is the habit with most of our litterateurs, seek to qualify the errors that his ignorance entails upon him, by the fertilitv and profusion of his abuse.

An eminent Journalist has seen a relapse into a

good style, after putting on a worse one for novelty. Now, for my life, I can neither see any change, nor am conscious of any affectation. It seems to me now, as at the beginning, a plain matter of setting down just such whimseys as pop into my brain, in good, old-fashioned English, available by every well-educated man, and which even the boarding-school mistresses cannot willfully set their faces against. The truth is, I suspect, that the critics and authors are so full of the tricks of literary metamorphose, both in opinion and style, that they have not the charity to give any new pen-man the credit of straight-forward honesty.

A friend (Sheridan would have called him devilish good-natured) was most earnest in his condemnation of the papers, as the flippant observations of a mere boy, who, he told me, was occasional contributor to a literary paper. Now, Heaven knows, that I have none but the most kindly feeling toward precocious literary boys; but if my paper is to be credited to any of them, I humbly entreat that they would try so far to improve their reputations, as to render the allegation no longer a hideous reproach.

I have ascertained, too, by occasional remark, which has been a sort of gauge to the current of literary criticism, that the town opinion is divided by coteries, each one of which thinks itself the special and heaven-appointed guardian of the national literary interests; and, as is quite natural and humane, each clique is tooth and nail against its fellow. Whatever is accomplished under the smiles of one, is reckoned the worst heresy by the other; and the two limbs of our most excellent Presbytery, or the 'Standing Committee' and the prayerful enemies of the Bishop, are not so sincerely and cordially at variance, as the literary coteries.

Now, as I am not acknowledged by any of them, I find myself kicked about unceremoniously by all; and am very much in the position of some unfortunately humble Christian, who gets a fisticuff from the Old School, because he refuses to send babies to perdition, and a slap from the New, because a partial believer in the old doctrine of Necessity; while he is heartily anathematized by the advance wing of the Mother Church, because he doubts the regenerating influence of Croton water, or has the impertinence to prefer a black gown to a white one.

It amuses me not a little, to watch the pretentious manner with which some middle-aged gentlemen condemn me; they wear a pretty air of authority, made good by the seductive smiles of admiring spinsters, and sustained by a large amount of apparent causticity and acumen. Such gentlemen are the inoffensive Nestors of large circles of very eager, and very moderately witted ladies. They cherish a certain cultivated frown, and condemn by a twist of the lip, and are very sure never to praise any who may come within hearing of their praise, or whose proximity might throw their own stature into the shade. I have been myself annihilated time and again by these gentlemen ; so that really the weekly placard in my publisher's window, has seemed to me an impertinence toward my critics, that has made me almost tremble for my temerity.

Yet they are worthy, kind fellows in a quiet way, doing little harm in the world, highly amusing to their indulgent friends, and critical enough for all dinner purposes; if they were ever to submit their observations to print, they would doubtless differ widely from those of the LORGNETTE. I should be very sorry, at any rate, to think otherwise.

There is another class of men who boast too a *nil admirari* air, who cultivate assiduously a habit of condemnation, and who maintain a great reputation with college boys, and under law-clerks, as 'cutting fellows.' They are akin to that school of politicians which is bent on equalizing, by pulling back the foremost. For them, nothing is good enough to be done; and nothing that is done, is well done. They quarrel incessantly with society, manners, and religion; they venture showers of regrets that nothing is done to amend them; at every new literary endeavor, they curl their lip;—yet they do nothing. God forbid, Fritz, that I should seem to urge them to any literary task, or to become the innocent cause of deluging the town with their efforts.

My only object is to give them this little mirror of themselves. They maintain character by assault: a sneer cannot be answered, therefore their arguments are sneers. They live by spoils: they are of a hybrid-hyena race, without much tooth, but a great deal of claw and howl: they dig at graves, where thoughts lie buried, and suck up with their toothless gums the putridity—leaving the bone behind.

Not a few ladies, 'town-bred,' have put to me the direct question of authorship: if such ladies had been blessed with a little more of the *politesse* of M. de Trobriand,* and I quote him below, they would

* "Il n'est que le voile de l'anonyme pour permettre ces allusions délicates qui trouvent toujours, quelqu' innocentes qu'elles soient, des

have spared a harmless old gentleman the sin of open denial, and been quit of a breach of propriety, which they have committed through ignorance. Where is their gentle blood? Let me warn them to the search.

Qui nos commorit 'melius non tangere!' clamo.

A little, truculent, round-eyed lady, who, as I am informed, has been practicing a thousand arts for a long period of years, to win notice, and to thrust herself among those she worships and hates—the people of the *ton*, has condemned my papers as silly and foolish, and its author as a stupid fellow. Softly, my dear Madam; indeed, you must not wince because I have unmasked your arts: by so doing, you will only individuate yourself among the innocent toadyists of our 'great:' and your disapproval, so far from weakening the reputation of my paper, will, I am sure, among those who know you best, add a laurel to my humble chaplet.

Another *ci-devant* belle, of worshipful memory, whose triumph-age has now passed, leaving to her few of the rational pleasures of the fireside, has told me that she thought the LORGNETTE very in-

consciences chatouilleuses toute prêtes à se gendarmer à la moindre piqûre, et quand on en use avec autant de discrétion, c'est *une curiosite blamable* que de s'efforcer d'en pénétrer le secret."—UN ŒIL A LA LORGNETTE sipid; and in an excess of indignation, had burned the numbers. She regretted that she had not provided herself with the 'Squints;' I joined cordially in her regret, and expressed myself certain, that the desired work would be much more to her taste. A belle *passée*, who has exhausted all moderate means of mental *excitation*, and whose vanities are sickening under the neglects that age brings in its train, has no resource but in the piquancy of ribaldry, or the grossness of open license. As the passions of our merely worldly women grow too faint for fleshly gratification, or their charms too small to ensure it, they will inevitably run toward the debauchery of books, and gloat over the lusts of the pen.

These prefatory sketches are not, my dear Fritz, foreign to my aim; they give you, well as anything can, an idea of the currents, and opinions of our town life. We will return now to our special portraitures.

THE FASHIONABLE LADY.

"The town as usual, met her in full cry;
The town as usual, knew no reason why."—CHURCHILL.

——"The husband or father, methinks, is like Ocnus in the fable, who is perpetually winding a rope of hay, and an ass at the end perpetually eating it."—COWLEY.

THE fashionable lady is born of reputable parents

—not always of genteel, or even respectable parents—but *reputable* ones. Her early years are passed variously between baby-jumpers, and wet-nurses. While at a tender age, she is taught the advantages of dress by becoming lessons, and by practice in very short petticoats, and very long white stockings, as well as a hat, shaped like an inverted slop-bowl, with proper quantity of ribbon and flowers—to match. She toddles out in frills, small sun-shade, and white gloves, with a shrewd nurse, who has an eye 'for folks what is folks;' and she may frequently be seen, with her nose curiously flattened against the window of her mother's coach.

She is taught early the impropriety of going out alone, or of democratic, and careless association with the neighbors' children. Her toy-books are well selected; and her library is specially rich in those, which, as the advertisement says, have given unfeigned delight to their numerous Royal Highnesses—the children of Victoria. By these the young fashionable lady is supposed to gain right ideas about aristocracy of sentiment, and courtly proprieties. She is, moreover, favored with the moral teaching and talking of a *femme de chambre*, nominally from Paris, but literally, and pronunciation-ly, from the Auvergne.

She is taught to look with proper languishment upon little fashionable boys, and makes early acquaintance with a cheap, second-story hair-dresser. She is taken to Grace Church in her best hat and gloves,—is pinched to kneel, and pinched again to incline herself prettily in the confession. She is told what a charming Christian place it is—is indoctrinated as to the ends and aims of such a delightful religious assembly-room, and is taught to look, with becoming feelings of pity, upon such poor outcast creatures as go to other churches.

She spends four years at school—the most expensive accessible—where she learns that Europe is quite populous and gay ;—that America is yet in its infancy ;—that republic is the name of our government ;—that Franklin drew down philosophy from heaven, with a small kite-string ;—that *tricotage* is of many sorts ; and that literature consists mainly of Tennyson's poems, Byron's tales, Shakespeare, Professor Longfellow, Tupper's Philosophy, and Mister Tuckerman.

She learns collaterally, that the French is the court language, and so, very desirable,—that the Latin is technically 'dead,'—that the waltz and polka are of the same family, and that the chief end of man is to get houses, and to behusband women. She is further taught, at a surprisingly early age, the nature and uses of fans, of beaux, of chemisettes, of gloves, the comparative effects of plaid and stripes, the disposition of cuffs, and the chemical nature of perfumery and amandine. She catches early at the distinction between moustache and whiskers, and has a correct general idea of sack-coats and imperials.

She is put, at a certain stage of her educational career, under the charge of some literary gentleman of quick wit and persuasive address, who expounds to her fine passages of the poets, and important epochs in history ; all which is presented in an attractive chit-chat shape, admirably adapted to the ends in view.

She graduates in a pretty hat, with a deft use of the fan, a passable familiarity with French table-talk, an Italian song or two, a smart capacity for purse-knitting, a general idea of the geographical divisions of the globe, and some few axioms of political economy :—such as, that money is necessary to luxury—that lace has a tendency to become soiled—that the best gloves are manufactured in Paris—that camphene will clean them, and that the law of divorce is a sort of moral make-shift.

Now comes on her age of practice,—practice of French talk, piano practice, practice of coquetries, waltzing practice, and Christian practice. In each of these she has practical professors, well taught, of the highest prices, and fully equal to their business. They will perfect a young lady of parts, in a surprisingly short time.

Her 'coming out,' if adroitly managed, will be a very taking card: it should not be too early or too late, and will depend much on the strength, height, and bodily capacity of the subject—on the views of the advising aunts, and on the comparative attractions and prospects of elder sisters. Thus, a female member of a family, who has reached the age of twenty-five, without inspiring any very tender emotions, would do well to keep a junior sister in pantalets, as long as propriety or prudery will allow. If fairly 'engaged' before the age specified, a year or two may be safely docked off from her sister's probationary, and small-girl state. In the case of several sisters whose looks are not killingly captivating, the youngest will be apt to fare like Cinderella in the ash-heap, and will run a sad chance of nursery-tails, and short dresses, up to an unfortunate maturity.

The 'coming out' will indeed sometimes depend on the mental development and age of the individual, and more rarely upon the common sense of the parties. Great preparations must be made, and assiduous efforts to secure the presence of certain well-known leaders of the ton. There will be conferences with Martel, and distinguished chaperon spinsters—to say nothing of those enterprising gentlemen, Messrs. Browne and Weller.

If the mamma has the misfortune to be merely respectable, the fashionable young lady will gain upon her by wide steps, and comes soon to regard her with due sentiments of pity. She instructs her mother as to what soirées she had better attend, and gives her discretionary advice about remaining in the corner. She puts forward all her powers of fascination, to attach to herself fashionable young men; and though at first, she will find herself obliged to dance with very indifferent persons who are 'not much in society,' she must yet be discreet in her refusals at this early stage of her career.

A little extra freedom in the waltz, if gracefully caught, will not harm her prospects, but will rather add a piquancy to her style, which if duly cultivated may come to counterbalance the most uninteresting face in the world. She should not be immeasurably shocked at any *double entendres* she may hear, but should credit them to a higher state of fashionable culture than she has yet reached. She might safely bear in mind, in this connection, the advice Madame de Sevigné gives her daughter: '*Tachez non enfant, de vous ajuster aux mœurs et aux manieres des gens avec qui vous avez à vivre; ne vous dégoutez point de ce qui n'est que mediocre; faites vous un plaisir de ce qui n'est pas ridicule.'*

As town fashion, like the town literature, is divided into numerous conflicting cliques, she would do well to select the most promising, and attach herself firmly to it. This she can easily do by lavishing very special praises upon all its members, and still better, by hearty abuse of any rival clique. It will not be reckoned indeed (as the opinion runs), any great sacrifice of dignity, if she should become the attachée of some enterprising lady of fashion, whose suppers are good, whose balls are splendid, whose religion is fair, and whose position is undoubted.

The summer campaign, if rightly directed, will be of essential service. She can easily ascertain, by a little careful observation, the probable current of the more fashionable 'sets;' and she will throw herself, inadvertently as it were, into the drift. The United States at Saratoga, the Ocean House at Newport, and the Pavilion of Sharon, are upon the whole safe places, and much may be effected in the incipient stages of fashionable growth, at either one. Still she must be careful of her times; a visit too early in the Summer might do her serious damage, and an arrival just previous to the height of the season will work capitally well.

She should be cautious, however, of meeting any shabby country friends at either place ; and to this end, should carry on an active correspondence for a week or two in advance, with her country cousins —engaging to meet them *late in the season.* A thin old lady in calico, who says, 'our folks,' or a young man who dresses in a flimsey, black dress-coat of a morning, who carries a baggy cotton umbrella, and who blows his nose on the 'stoop,' with a 'silk handkercher,' might do her serious damage.

She should also be quite sure that she will not be overtopped,—that is, that she will not be 'cut' by any established *habitué ;* rather than expose herself to such deterioration, she would do well to postpone her visit. If the Papa, in any matter-of-fact way, sets his face against an expenditure he cannot afford, and proves deaf to all entreaties for the 'Springs,' she must change her tactics ; in that case she would do well to speak deprecatingly of the fashionable places, as being altogether 'too mixed,'—drop hints about barbers, and bar-tenders in moustache,—'no knowing who one will fall in with,'—'for her part she cannot bear it!' If this is well executed, it will be very telling.

If a fancy ball should take place within her permission, she will select such dress as bears a fair stamp of gentility, by having been already honored with the wearing of some lady of distinction. She will farther, by dint of a few coy and well-covered hints to a gentleman friend, who knows the Express writers, accidentally make their acquaintance; and then, her Saracco and boudoir education has been surely very poor, if she do not so beguile the poor devils with her dance and smiles, as to secure for herself a charming period about taper ancles, and bust of Hebe, which will, of course, set her up for the winter.

Her preparatives for the town season must be directed with care and energy. Dress, she should be slow to decide upon until the 'leaders' have given their orders; and by a proper intimacy (spiced with free use of money) with Miss Lawson, she will learn in advance what Mesdames So-and-so have ordered, and will, by a singular coincidence, hit upon the same. No wide difference from the popular standard will be advisable, unless indeed, the lady set up for an eccentric, or have recently returned from abroad; and even in the latter case, there will be needed a strong savor of previous respectability, and good connections, to legitimatize any outré trimmings of either hat or cloak. With the vantage ground, however, of established position, an extravagance will be smiled upon, and the 'second rates' will be taught by conspicuous example, that the popular idea, that Paris ladies adapt their fashions of dress to the style of the wearer, is a great mistake.

The Opera must not be forgotten; whatever may be one's love of music, it would be well to cultivate a slight knowledge of the operatic art, a familiarity with the more popular pieces, and effective criticisms upon the different musical composers. If the fashionable lady has been abroad, all this will be at once presumed, and her air of indifference will be the most naïve in the world. She must, moreover, secure a bevy of tonnish visitors at her box; nothing short of it will sustain her rank. For instance, it would be well to make sure *d'avance* of at least one unmistakeable moustache, one journalist, one foreigner, one 'handsome' man, one 'clever' man, one young professional man of creditable position, and a husband who is understood to be on uneasy terms with his wife. A boy in wide white cravat may be treated with provoking carelessness; and a polka dancer of doubtful grace, should be met with equal indifference. A country cousin, who happens to be in town, should be tolled off with a free ticket to a concert.

If sure of the place, and has seen a particular air

applauded at the Queen's Theatre, she may clap her hands, when all around are gossiping; unless indeed, some lady of foreign birth should be near, who would remark the exception. The fashionable lady, if well instructed, will not be astonished at any strange burst of music, or any eccentricities of the singers. Indeed, she will never manifest surprise, except when saluted cordially by some lady of an under set. She will look patronizingly toward young ladies of 'family,' and regard only through her opera-glass, the beauties who are not yet 'in society.'

After a winter or two of such experience, and an open acquaintance with gentlemen of acknowledged fashion, she can cast off the leading string of her chaperons, and live her own life of fashion, as proudly, and reasonably independent, as the belly-full beggar in the play;—

> Non ego nunc parasitus sum, sed regum rex regalior;
> (Tantus ventri commeatus meo adest in portu cibus.)*

Meantime, she is not supposed to be insensible (few ladies are) to the virtues and necessities of a husband. Three seasons of single life display, if the face wears well, are the minimum for a fashiona-

* Plautus, Capteivei, iv. 2. The clever critic of the Literary World, who has detected in my papers a classical inaccuracy, will correct me if I am wrong, and will confer a special favor by multiplying his 'instances' of 'bad citations.'

ble lady ; and as for the maximum, I fear I should offend some very tender friends of mine, by even hinting at its period.

When the matter, however, really becomes serious, there must be a concentration of effort on the part of our fashionable lady, to which her past life has been altogether a stranger. It will not do at all to retain the old flippancy when talking with bald-headed bachelors of a certain age, who are understood to be living on 'their means.'

It will be well, moreover, to practice a little self-denial in the polka, and not wear so languishing an air with the young bucks, when the marriageable gentlemen are looking on. She may even venture, on extraordinary occasions, to abandon the polka altogether, and her church virtues (not always Christian ones) should, in view of marriage, be punctiliously attended to. Of course, she will have a running knowledge of 'expectancies,' and will detect easily how far the candidate is of a compliant and yielding disposition. A little eminence of position by marriage with a lion, is not to be overlooked by the fashionable lady ; but if she have sober judgment in the matter, she will see that it is infinitely better to become the lion herself, by overtopping the husband, and by possession of abundant means.

Having through papa negotiated the preliminary terms of a 'brilliant match,' she appears at careless exhibitory intervals, upon the public walks of the town, never forgetting herself so much as to show a spark of enthusiasm, and never so natural as to indulge in regrets.

The wedding is the occasion for picking up and cementing together, by engraved reception cards, the dispersed fashionable elements which belong to the respective 'sets' of both parties. The ceremony must not be without its *èclat*. The bridal presents, disposed with a proper eye to our growing Republican magnificence, will make the talk of the boudoir and salon; and the lace veil of the church, and some manifest extravagances of dress, will give chat material to gaping lookers-on, and the showy finish to a 'City Item.'

And yet, Fritz,—such is the *morale* of our town—you shall find that this very item eulogist, who will panegyrize the splendor of the ceremony, the magnificence of the dresses, the style of the equipages, to purchase a familiar nod, or possibly an invitation to a 'crush' of the winter, will, in his private mood, vapor lustily against the town-worship of wealth, and the bestiality of that appreciation which measures everything by its capacity for display. Such is the sincerity and purpose of our censors of public taste; bowing the Baal knee to every manifestation of wealth, where the obeisance may stand them in small stead, and loosening their pent-up vanities only in the bar-rooms, and in the street, against the wretched artificiality of our distinctions. In private, they are cynics; and in print, the veriest lick-spittles of us all!

God forbid, Fritz, that you in your luxurious country quarters, should see in all this, a covert sneer at wealth; in our country it must long be, and properly is a great measurer of force; and by force, I mean character, talent, activity, and mental leverage. It is the forerunner, too, of those comforts and that indulgence which give time and room for cultivation; it is the grand furnace-warmer of those nursery-beds from which sprout up the tropical crop of refined luxuries. But in Heaven's name, let us honor it, for what it is, and not for what it is not; most of all, let us avoid that particular fallacy which sees in wealth the essence, and not the provocative of refinement.

It would be invidious, as well as fill too much space, to say how many in our town are essentially and brutally vulgar, in the possession of ample fortune: how many are making brilliant show with equipages and with coats-of-arms—listening with fashionable earnestness to the hand-organ-like lectures of Mr. Lord, and who are yet as ignorant of Abelard as of modesty, and whose library books are but painted backs. What would you say, too, to foul crockery and cotton napkins, within a palace of freestone, or to the vulgarity of that wealth, which seeks only the outward and flagrant means of addressing the money-worshiping eye, and which is satisfied with the stare and livery of ignorant coachmen, as the most grateful incense to its deity, and with the sickly mention of pamphleteers and newspaper item, as the sweetest token of its honor?

It would be odious, too, to mention how much of this very pabulum that feeds display, has been gained by most deceptive practices—not, indeed, coming within the court calendar of villanies, but that worthier and more honorable list of chicaneries, which are too mean to have been anticipated by law-givers, and which even our New Code men, with all their quickness at littlenesses, did not believe the race to have been capable.

To be sure, there is a hatred of wealth, due to the smallest of our litterateurs, who boast of refinement without possessing any trace of that fine soul-thread of gentleness, running with every nerve, and which constitutes the life-artery of thorough breeding. This I will cordially join you in condemning, and with God's help, will do what is in my power to dissipate that prurient affectation of superiority, which the reading of current books, familiarity with newspaper columns, and an unscholarly handling of the pen induces—but which is without the saving virtue of that high and true soul-refinement, which must lie deep-seated in the man—which must have had its office in every step of his education, and in every shadow of his action; and which will make his bearing and his words as unmistakeable as the presence of genius.

But we are losing sight of our fashionable lady. With marriage, her best life of show is only begun. She can now run riot in a thousand frivolities without periling her chance. Her ambition, which before may have been bounded by some vague traditions of virginal delicacy, is now wide in its range. Yet withal she will be punctilious in her church duties; she may even wear a matronly air; and will be specially coy of manifesting any vulgar attachment to her husband or household. She is now mistress of her establishment, and it will be the fault or failing of her husband's commerce, if it do not shine with all those attractions which decoy the vagrant peacocks of the hour.

A little whispered license will add zest to her company, and bring her *sociale* nearer to the Parisian standard. Perhaps a European tour, by post, a smuggled ticket to Torlonia's, ana a cultivated intimacy with such Paris society, as will welcome money, and will pay in the loose coin of social teaching, and the piquant equivoques of conversational intrigue, will open her eyes wider to the mysteries and delights of higher fashion

Perhaps with some faint remnants of a better feeling, tracing its beginnings to a comparatively harmless childhood, she will sigh at the vanities which surround her, and the deceptions which mock the little sense of truth that remains;* but there is no escape; the distinguished husband, the leader of the ton, has got no ear for the foolish confidences of a repining lady, or for the sharp-uttered sentiments of disgust, which their common life has ripened. She is bound by brazen bands to a set—the first set—which has demands upon her, unceasing and regular, for her quota of the stimuli of fashionable action.

So she lives, staving off age long as she can, with all the appliances of a quickened and nervously unquiet ingenuity; but time will press her, and will, before long, strand her withered and colorless hulk upon the beach of age; her silken sails will flap idly against the rotting spars, and will fill no long-

* The kind letter of a lady correspondent, *apropos* to this topic, is thankfully acknowledged. John Timon presents his best compliments, and will be happy to hear from her farther.

er under the breath of fashionable applause; all the kedges of her golden cables will not drag her back to the stream of popular favor.

At length she dies; she is buried by the gentlemanly sexton, who has so ably superintended her parties; she is honored, perhaps, with a patent metallic sarcophagus, and goes—where?

Where should she go (if it is not impertinent to ask), to culminate that life which has had its careful beginnings here? Where shall she mature those projects of town rank, those pretty polka devices, those studies of street display, which have been the aim of her mortal wishes? I wonder if the pretty light of the Grace Church windows will reach high enough to light her, or the carriages at the door be stanch enough to carry her, of themselves, all the way to heaven? The Devil, surely, with all his malice, will not overlook the claims of those who have been laboring through a long life for a position in the 'first society;' and he will, without doubt, give invitations for the most *recherché* of his evening parties, to very many of our 'leaders of the ton.'

Seriously, Fritz,—what benevolence, what rational action, what generous self-denying endeavor, will help our fashionable lady toward that species of future happiness which, however the

Doctors may disagree, is very sure not to be made up precisely, of Forti's singing, or Saratoga Springs? Under which item of the 'Sermon on the Mount' shall we reckon her dawning chances? Upon what text shall the Doctor preach her funeral eulogy? John Timon offers this from the Psalms;—(and if the Doctors were as honest as they are politic, they could not find a better)—'*They have dreamed out their dream, and awakening, have found nothing in their hands!*'

I leave it all, Fritz, the text, the woman, and the 'improvement,' to the preacher;—not the elegant preacher of a fashionable assemblage, nor the respectable preacher of a Presbyterian hierarchy, nor the absolution of a political Bishop, nor the moral novels of a seceding clergyman, but with the best preacher of all—the individual conscience. And if our fashionable lady has not smothered his talk already, let her listen while she can.

This is uncommonly sober talk, my dear Fritz, for an Opera-goer; but, remember, that we are breathing now in the breast of Lent; and the gray hairs, and the fleeting time warn me, that such talk may not 'fall to the ground,' even in the careless pages of a gossiping essayist.

TIMON.

APRIL 4. NEW-YORK. NO. 10.

"As in geometry, the oblique must be known, as well as the right; and in arithmetic, the odd as well as the even; so in actions of life, who seeth not the filthiness of evil, wanteth a great foil to perceive the beauty of virtue."—SIR PHILIP SIDNEY.

"MR. TIMON:—I am astonished at you, my dear sir; why do you speak so harshly of the town ladies, and present them in so unfavorable lights? I have been all along a most excellent friend to your paper, and have, time and again, defended you against most merciless assaults; but if you do not speedily amend, and speak better of us, I shall leave you to defend yourself.

"Yours indignantly,

"A LADY."

This little fragment of a letter touches me tenderly, and shall have a full and courteous notice; which, if it do not serve as vindication of my action, will at least certify to my well-disposed correspondent, the influence of her advices, and the honesty of my disposition.

You, my dear Fritz, will I am sure be greatly surprised to find me, who have been so long, and untiringly the devoted friend, and admirer of the gentler sex, suddenly become the object of their frowns and animadversions. It is but poor remuneration, surely, for a life spent in devotional exercises toward the reigning half of Christendom, to find myself subjected to the imputation of libelous assault, and to the most heinous of all charges — that of lack of gallantry. When you recall, Fritz, my Quixotic career, scattered over as it has been, with innumerable hazards, and such hair-breadth escapes, as would have done honor to the hero of La Mancha, or Santillane, you will smile to think that any should be hardy enough to impugn the action of my maturer age, and to credit to unworthy motives, those whimsical observations of mine, which are half made up of irony, and half of covert praise. You will recognize the apparent acerbity as only the occasional and delirious excess of the fever of a life-long gallantry— the accidental and interrupted lance-thrusts of an old knight who trembles in his stirrups, and whose blow is rendered only the more uncertain by reason of the warmth of his blood, and the ecstasy of his admiration.

True regard does not gloss over errors in the objects of its attachment, but rather by judicious mention of such as appear, seeks to win them away from their occasional sinnings, and make them worthier of that respect which grows by witness of reform, and which covets excellence.

I have spoken, it may be, somewhat harshly, and in castigating humor (if such humor can be predicated of a mild old gentleman's remark) of many of the ways of the fashionable ladies of the hour; and if I have been a little extravagant, it was only in the hope of frighting away from the worst vanities of the town life, by exhibiting them through the magnifying lenses of my glass. And even supposing all to be real and unexaggerated,—about which point I foresee that there will be much difference of opinion,—yet I should in no whit blame myself for the representation, but rather be emboldened by the conviction, that I should still possess the sympathies of those who suffer, the compassion of those who are blinded, and the cordial dislike of those who are guilty. Nor are the times or opinions so corrupt, but that these should prove very clever supports to any man who earnestly seeks them. I know that I could sleep very quietly upon them, and with a conscience 'void of offence.'

But have I a right, in remarking upon the untruth, and frivolities of the social life in the city, to bear so hardly, and so pertinently upon the ladies of the town?

Most unquestionably: and in saying this, I do them honor;—at least, such small honor as can be reaped from the admission, that in energy, influence, and activity, they are vastly before any of those milliner gentry, calling themselves men, who affect to set the rules, or to sway the fashions for our social guidance. Who, pray, transfers the *spectacle* from the stage, to the boxes of our Opera; who sustains the drunken etiquette of the ball-room; who favors, by toleration, study, and practice, the most questionable of the foreign polkas; who smiles upon the most needless of display, and makes a parquette of pews; who gives a boy-tone to the salon-talk; who fulminates the scandal, and befriends the laced lacqueys? Who has translated Mr. Browne—the new Enoch (not Una)—from the funereal escutcheon of his undertaker's employ, to the 'heaven of invention'—invention of ball-room tickets, and ball supplies; who has transmuted thriving school-boys into rapt polkists ; who is arranging our marriages for convenience, and our houses for mere display ? Are not our town ladies ordering these things to their own taste ; who else is competent ? Will they not agree with me in saying, that sensible men are not weak enough, and that men without sense are not strong enough?

We, in our country, Fritz, have long given a supremacy to the Eve section of the human family, which has grown into a national characteristic. We have become the troubadours, and knights errant of the nineteenth century chivalry. It is an American distinction. The rush and fever of business which 'steeps to the ears' nine out of ten of our men, has indeed made the obeisance (the gallantry if you please) a necessity ; nevertheless, it exists, and is insisted on. Gynocracy, to use the nomenclature of a literary man, is the disorder of the town; and the old *anthropocracy* (to humor the critic's classical conceit) is known only to the business alleys of the city.

Women are clearly responsible, then, for whatever abuses obtain in our social life. They fix our hours of sleep, of eating, dancing, and worship. They make the rules of our receptions; they give the formulas for the interchange of hospitalities; they establish the ages of beaux and belles, upon a basis somewhat similar to Sir Robert Peel's 'Sliding scale;' they give a character to our music and our polkas; they rectify and sublimate our devotions. They give the cue, even, to education, and point out the limits of mental attainment. In most of these, and specially the last, they are easy masters, not pushing us into much erudition, nor wearying us with the imposition of much reading; nevertheless, they are in all that relates to the social intercourse of life, our lawgivers and taskmasters. The old Italian proverb, '*l'uomini sono azioni; le donne sono voci,*' is now reversed: women are deeds, and men, words.

If, then, we, their subordinates in these matters, do sometimes suggest inquiry, or question action, let them not take advantage of their superior position to bear us down ignominiously, and silence us by their frowns. Let them be generous as they are strong; and suffer a quiet gentleman to throw out such observations as his enfeebled sense may suggest, without condemning him altogether, and putting him to the pillory of their critiques.

I do not at all mean to imply the necessary ill-effects, or the unnaturalness of any such state of lady-government. Social life, next to domestic (about which it is unfashionable to talk in the city), is the woman's proper province. The affections and passions which belong to her, are its arbiters. Without her ballot, the most refined are outcasts, and with it, the most slavish are admissible. Even our respected friend Mr. Browne owes his adroitness only to a right judgment of her whimseys, and by really humoring, while he seems to advise. The gracious sexton is not unworthy the title of his old namesake, Tom. Browne.

The ladies rate the standing of every in-coming family, and discuss and arrange the chances of its position. Mercantile connections, and all the club favors of gentlemen, are nothing to the familiar reception of an accredited lady. It is only necessary for an aspirant after social distinction, to be taken 'by the hand' of some notoriously well-known lady, and *presto*, he finds himself transformed, as quickly as the balls under a conjuror's cup, from red to white, or from white to red. He may woo, sigh, and grow faint of heart at the first, without so much as the nod of a dowager's plume to his earnest salutations; but let him once have the public recognition of an umpire of the taste, and his rusticity will grow into an eccentric refinement, and he will be the mark for a multidude of favors from the 'middlings,' and of smiles from the well-taught.

Even John Timon has to avow his gratitude

to those who have extended to him the helping hand, and who, notwithstanding the sneers of the Journals, have introduced his paper to the favor of elegant society; (and this, surely, not because I have tickled their vanity!) It takes off certainly, not a little from the face of the compliment, to know that the most *gauche*, and splay-footed of cockneys have been set up in the same way, and that the character of those who get the *accolade* of fellowship is not of so much importance, as their bearing upon the boudoir tattle. What is talked of, must be known.

And this brings me, Fritz, to a most ungracious branch of my subject; not only are our town ladies the arbiters of all social form, (as indeed they properly should be,) but they are also gifted by nature with a certain happy love of display; nor has nature in this regard been improvidently left to neglect, but has shot up, under judicious culture, into a yearning after distinctions, and a ripeness of vanity, as much superior to that of men, as to that of beasts. In this, too, they maintain their established eminence; with the worse sort, it breeds the mercenary loves, the winks at vulgarity and ignorance; and with the better, it creates tolerance for manifest extravagances, and an easy conscience under the coming reign of surplice, and confessional, and the prettiest ceremonials of imported Romanism. This has set the heraldic panels to our carriages; this has tricked our coachmen in liveries; and this is making our children reverent of courtly display.

Town ladies make very poor democrats. They are not tending toward any Greeley philosophy of equality, but are cutting us up into sets, which, if their theories mature, will ripen into aristocratic castes. I do not mean to hint, Fritz, that I am a believer in any Proudhonic system of social democracy, or that superior refinement will not always make itself distinct by elevation, as surely and as unconsciously as Saturn burns brighter than the smallest of the asteroids. But this token of superiority is not reckoned in the schedule of our modes; we fetch over instead such poor pickings from the wardrobe of foreign rank, as will serve the vanities of wealth, and not offend too openly the hurly-burly vanity of the street. Exclusion is a far better security for eminence than .cultivation. Let me throw it out, then, to the ladies, who have the power in their hands (though it may seem like a bit of stolidity, and mock seriousness,)—if it is not better after all, to cultivate the dignity of the Roman matron, or the fidelity of the Spartan mother, though they were not crowned with jewels, than to study, and ape those brilliancies, which made the honor of a Maintenon, and the virtue of a De l'Enclos?

The Journalists may vapor as they will, and the clergy talk milk-and-water regrets, spreading their sanctimonious admonitions softly on the heads of respectable churches; yet if the women, in whose hands the matter lies, do not waken their action, while they gild their creeds, admonitions and vapors will prove but waste wind. If the ladies of ton will doat on boobies in their teens, they may rest assured that the town will continue to furnish an unfailing supply; if they will glory in gorgeousness of equipage, the saddle men will thrive; if their conversation lowers itself to the capacity of school-boys, they will always be sure of devout listeners; if belleship is measured by polking; and refinement by opera-going, and blarney about Benedetti, there will never be lack of belles, and never a short cross of refinement. Honors are easily worn which cost nothing in the getting; and that cultivation will be easily sustained, whose only proof and issue is a noisy claim of possession. Ridiculous assumptions, and foolish foppery will never expire, while they have the tender fondling of lady-mothers.

The merchant might be content with his princely mansion, comfortably garnished with all the appliances for bed, books, and board ; but the lady must astonish her opposite neighbors, by the magnificence of her curtains, and must ransack Marley's or Baudouine, for some bit of furniture more outré than any in the possession of her very dear friend Madame Somebody else. The husband might possibly be contented with moderate festivity among his friends ; but our Juno of the salon snubs her much attached Jove, and distresses him with a houseful of curiously-gathered lions. The father might be satisfied with a wholesome education for his daughter, throwing out the newest of the polkas, and the making of sonnets ; but the Mamma overrules, and encourages cultivation by the most modern of the dances, perseverance by the latest of the hours, and humility by the lowest of the low-necked dresses. The 'old gentleman' might keep his son at study until he is firm upon his legs, and show some signs of beard ; but our elegant lady must push him early at Saracco's, and gratify her motherly ambition with his proficiency in the ball-room, and by the professional praises of Mr. Browne.

The husband, poor fellow, might have some taste for what used to be called domestication, with his hopeful son, and his polking daughter, at his side ; but the concerts, operas, balls, and Broadway promenades have arranged it for him otherwise ; if he admires, he must admire where they most study to be admired ; and if he rebels, he will very likely be compelled to bury his rebellion at the club, and cheer himself with a cigar, and the yesterday's papers. He will have no more hand in forming the tastes or character of his daughter, than our hero Martel, or the most assiduous of the polka dancers.

And here, Fritz, I come upon another topic, which it will be ungrateful to handle. Womanly eminence in our day and town is turned away from the hearth, and runs riot in the streets. What lady can be found so silly as to aspire to the distinction of being a good housekeeper, affectionate mother, or tender wife? What one, so short-sighted as not to sigh for the reputation of showing the latest modes, of appreciating the most worthless opera, or of driving the most stylish equipage?

Praise is no longer looked for at home, but in the world. Merit is reckoned by the club-room babble and the newspaper 'item.' Contempt of less things grows naturally upon the love of the greater and noisier. Dash is worth more than virtue; town-talk is better than the commendation of a friend. To achieve position in a set, where the position shall have public recognition, is an aim dearer to hundreds of our hopeful ladies, than any domestic and worthy nobility. The old-fashioned notion that a woman's throne might be built up highest at home is exploded ; publicity is the testimony to her honor, and the end of her ambition. The Lucretias are growing rare, while the Tarquins are thickening. The Lares are transplanted from the fireside, and are set up, like the painted images in Papal Switzerland, at the shop windows, and street corners. The only vestal fire to be heard of, is in the blaze of the opera chandelier.

Our 'leaders of ton' do not care so much to please, as to astonish, and had rather bewilder by the multiplication of etiquette, than attract by its simplicity. John Timon takes the liberty of telling them, that in this they steer as wide of good breeding as of kind intent. Mackenzie says, somewhere—'A great man may perhaps be well-bred in a manner which little people do not understand ; but trust me, he is a greater man who is well-bred in a manner that everybody understands.'

What do we derive from all this, Fritz ? First, that the ladies of our town have the control of our social life ; second, that their native vanity is not shocked at the consciousness of the power ; and third, that that vanity is unfortunately wedded to a publicity that braves modesty, begets scandal, and beggars morals.

Nor shall I allow myself to be condemned for this judgment, without bringing testimony for its support; and such testimony can surely be found in this letter which has come to hand within the week past, and in which I waive the equivocal compliment its author has paid me, for the truth and sincerity of the subject matter.

MR. TIMON:

DEAR SIR,—I do not know but a serious letter will be out of place amid the ironical talk, and only half-earnest tone of your paper; at any rate, I have determined to tell you what I think and feel—a thing I scarce ever do even to my husband. For I have been married, you must know, nearly three years; and for the last seven years we have been trying (my Mamma and I) to 'get up' in New York society. And now (Papa got rich four years ago last May) we have done it.

At first we had a small house in Thompson street, and I took lessons from Signor Piccolino twice a week on the guitar: I learned French at school. Mamma was very kind to the girls of 'good families' who went to our school, and used to ask them to come and take tea with me. Mamma always hired a new carriage at the stable near us, and told me not to take one with a number on it.

As Papa got richer we moved into Bleecker street, only two doors from Mrs. ——, who was of the 'first set.' We patronized her butcher, and used to ask the baker's boy what cakes and bread she took in. We studied her style of dress, and commenced walking Broadway. Papa changed my teacher, and got one for a higher price, though he was not so good as the other. We got a handsome German to teach me music, and I used to read Willis' poems, and Tupper's Philosophy: I got some of Willis' poems by heart, and they *are* sweet; so is Tupper.

We had little soirées now and then: at first there were hardly any gentlemen but papa's clerks, and cousin Dick, whom he would invite, though mamma didn't wish to. I took private lessons in polking, and used to get cousin Dick to come in mornings and practice with me. Papa got occasionally upon the committee for some public dinner, and mamma kept the paper that contained the account lying about handy.

We commenced soon making calls, and got on very well, though some of them were never returned; of course we cut them afterward. I liked reading pretty well, but couldn't get any time. Mamma told me not to waste my study on what was never talked of, and now since we take the Home Journal she says there's no excuse for not knowing just what to read.

We got some nice gentlemen to call on us after we had been in Bleecker street awhile: mamma flattered them, and papa gave them cigars when they went away. They didn't do much as I could learn, but were members of the club, and used to dance—oh—exquisitely. We dressed finely, and got to be friends with Miss Lawson: mamma talked about a carriage, but papa thought it would be better to get on 'by degrees.'

Pretty soon we moved up town and set up a carriage in earnest. I got new teachers, and paid them more than ever. We went to Saratoga, and my dress at the fancy ball was praised in all the papers. I couldn't walk down Broadway between three and four without getting twenty bows. Papa was very rich, and mamma began to be invited all about. We kept a man-servant, and had him wear white gloves at dinner parties, and on reception days. I purchased of Mr. Crowen some beautiful books for the centre-table, and everybody said we were getting to be fashionable. Mamma would smile and say 'oh no,' and, perhaps, say some hard things about fashionable people, as if they were not worth knowing, but she never meant them; and I, for my part, never said them. I forgot to tell you that we took a box at the Opera, and bought a half dozen lorgnettes. Our carriage was a pretty one, and our coachman wore—oh—ever so many capes.

I could get on very well in French, and had begun to get a little Italian, so that I could read with a dictionary a little of the Promessi Sposi. Still there were some sets we couldn't get into. Mamma thought it would be best to go to Europe; so we went. We traveled post all over the Continent. We made up a party at Rome with some titled people to go and see the Vatican statuary at night; and papa paid for all the torches. Little Clark got us into Torlonia's great ball; and at Naples we had splendid rooms at the Victoria, looking out on the *Villa Reale*.

I learned Italian as fast as I could, and bought lots of tortoise-shell, and lava ornaments, to give away when I came back.

Well, we spent two years so, and then came home. Papa gave grand dinner parties, and I believe our return was mentioned in the Express, and papa subscribed for the paper. We went to all the balls, and looked so 'knowing' at the Opera.

The gentlemen came to see me, and I had ever

so many flirtations: until one day mamma said I had better get married. You must not expect me to tell you if any of those we chose, 'played off:' it is enough to say that at length one, a pretty man, of good family, but without much money, was married to me.

It was very gay at the first; and 'the family' were very kind; and mamma said I might consider myself among the 'ton.' I dare say I am, but it don't seem such a great thing, after all.

And what is worse, everybody knows me, and all about our history. Husband says he don't like Tupper's Philosophy, so that I can't entertain him with books. And he don't speak French very easily, so we can't practice together; and when I ask him to dance, he says 'Pshaw! you are a simpleton!' yet he always dances with the married ladies at the balls. Mamma visits us occasionally to look over the card-basket, and tell me what a fine establishment I have got; and the clergyman comes, and says I ought to be very happy; and I suppose I ought; though somehow I am not.

It does seem to me that this sort of life is not, after all, very satisfying. To be sure it's very silly, but I cry sometimes. In Lent especially it was very dull; husband at the club, and no parties.

Can't you tell me, Mr. Timon, now that I have

been so honest with you, how I can amuse myself? Pray do, and if you choose you may print my letter, but don't let any one see the hand-writing.

Truly yours, AMANDA MIGGS *neé* DIGGS.

P.S.—My papa is getting up in the world: he is just building a long block, which he means to call Fitz-Diggs Block. Sweet name, isn't it?

I know not how to give advice on so serious a matter as my correspondent has here broached, without a more attentive consideration than I am now able to bestow. She may rest assured, however, that the subject shall not pass from my mind without mature reflection, and such attention from the LORGNETTE as its importance demands.

THE BOSTONIAN.

"*Cogitationes* hominum seqūntur plerunque *inclinationes* suas; *sermones* autem, *doctrinas* et *opiniones*, quas imbiberunt; At *Facta* eorum ferme *antiquum obtinent.*"—LORD BACON.

IT takes a vast deal to drive a man's habit or his nature out of him; the English philosopher says as much in his quaint Latinity. From this it follows, my dear Fritz, that all you see in New York are not New Yorkers. Neither tailors, nor hair-dressers, nor the club-talk, can so transform a man but that you shall see in him the lees of the *ancient*. Indeed, between the Hotels, the Opera-house, and the street, our town is not a bad point from which to study the characteristics of the nation.

The people of the Town are not destitute of a modicum of charity, and look with feelings of proper Christian benevolence upon all strangers, of whatever cut; while at the same time they wear an air of what seems most natural and unconscious superiority. But I observe that this is so carefully concealed, that the greater part of strangers, especially those from the neighbor cities, do not see it at all; and are apt to flatter themselves into the belief that they are passing current in the street throng, as indigenous and unadulterated specimens. Indeed, none but a Bostonian would ever resent being taken for a New Yorker; and so carefully do they of the sister city guard their identity by dress, action, and speech, that none but the most careless observer would ever affront them with the charge.

The Bostonian is strongly impressed with the idea that his city is the particular nucleus of all that there is great on this side of the Atlantic. He looks upon other American towns as small planetary bodies revolving about the centre of Boston Common, and deriving most of their light, heat,

THE BOSTONIAN.

and strength from Cambridge University, Fanueil Hall, and Boston Harbor. He affects a wonderful degree of kinship with the English ; and keeps up the connection by sharp shirt collars, short-waisted coats, and yellow gaiters. He is apt to put himself upon English stilts to look down upon the rest of the American world, which he regards complacently through an English eye-glass. He does not so much pity the rest of the American world, as he patronizes and encourages. His literary tastes being formed in the focus of western learning, are naturally correct and profound. He squats himself upon the Boston formulas of judgment, from which nothing can shake him, and puts out his feelers of opinion, as you may have seen a lazy, bottle-tailed bug try his whereabouts, without once stirring, by means of his glutinous and many-jointed antennæ.

He likes to try you in discussion, in the course of which it will be next to impossible to tell him anything that he did not previously know ; and you will prove a rare exception, if he does not tell you many things that you never knew before—unless, indeed, you have been in Boston. His stock of praises is uncommonly small, and principally reserved for home consumption ; things are done *well*, only in Boston ; though they are sometimes *creditably* done in other parts of the world.

His superiority in arts, letters, science, and religion, of which he will endeavor strenuously to convince one, is attributable partially to education, but mainly to his being a Bostonian. Whatever idea, or system of ideas, whether in politics, arts, or literature, which had not its beginning, or has not had its naturalization in Boston, is a fungous growth upon the great body of American opinion, which must of necessity wither and perish.

The Bostonian entertains the somewhat singular notion that whatever he has never observed, is not worth observing; and that the very few matters of fact and fancy scattered about the country, which are unbeknown to Bostonians, are not worth their knowing. This gives him under all ordinary circumstances a self-possession, and dignity of address which is quite remarkable. He does not conceive it possible that classical scholarship should thrive at all, out of sight of the belfry of the old South Church; and such chance citations from classic authors, as may appear on pages printed in other parts of the country, he considers filched in some way out of Boston books. He regards all those making any profession of learning, out of his own limits, very much as an under pedagogue will eye a promising boy of the 'first form' who occasionally hears recitations.

He plumes himself specially on his precision and exactness ; you will never see a Bostonian with the lower button of his waistcoat uncaught, and he is uniformly punctual to his dinner hour. Vivacity he condemns from principle—and the best of all principle, which is—Boston principle. Even in religion, he does not recognize the hot zeal of earnest intention, nor does he run toward the lusts of ceremonial. He is coy to acknowledge even the *personnel* of a Divine Mediation ; his dignity does not like to admit a superior between himself and the Highest. The comparative chilliness of the Unitarian faith suits the evenness of his temper ; and when he casts loose from this unique doctrine, which is to many a pure and holy faith, he runs inevitably into the iciness of Pantheism.

In politics he is Bostonian. He speaks lightly of the French, and of French Republicanism, and indeed of most sorts of Republicanism which are not reducible immediately or remotely to Boston Republicanism. He has a very tender charity, too, for the gross legal tyranny of his ancestral English ; and such of his sympathies as ramify beyond his Pontine marshes, or the Roxbury plains, clasp stoutly round the mosses and blotches of the royal oak of Britain.

In manners he is true to his faith; he walks stiffly, dances stiffly, and bows stiffly. Like the Englishman, he assimilates little with those among whom he may chance to fall: he guards his integrity by exception. His idea of elegance centres in precision; and the ease that he possesses is never more than familiarity. He is, like the Virginian, usually of an 'old family;' whoever heard of any other sort of families in the Old Dominion, or the 'Cradle of Liberty'?

The Bostonian sneers at the riff-raff of New York society, and will sometimes put a clever edge upon his sneers. He is the favorite of such ladies as love bookish talk, and who will not worry at an awkward polka. He is quicker at a bargain than a waltz, and he counts his town-talent a fair offset to the money and the graces of our belles. *A lui le talent,—à nos femmes la fortune; tout cela peut se marier.* He reads the Boston Atlas, and Boston books; he sighs for Boston Common; and lunches on Boston crackers.

All this, it must be understood, my dear Fritz, is predicated upon such stray specimens as may be seen here and there wandering down our streets, or adorning the corners, at our balls. That there is very much worthiness, that is here unnoted, about the race which belongs to Boston, the world knows. And if I were to make a particularity that should have its point, I would say that the admirable police, and municipal regulations of the sister city, its well-ordered pavements and well-swept streets, are worthy of all commendation, and much copy. And the Bostonian may well boast, that while our City Fathers are lazily drinking their tea in sight of our city desolation, that snug Eastern Seaport is gaining upon us by forced marches in all the commoner and most comfortable types of an advanced civilization.

As for the vagrant Bostonian, with whom I began, and who brings his *doctrinas*, and his *antiquum* with him, it is sincerely to be hoped that he will in time fall away from the greatness of his unbelief; and be willing to credit that eyes, heart, tongue, and brain have been mercifully vouchsafed to people in various parts of the world, by the same kind Providence which has so overstocked Boston Town.

TIMON.

APRIL 11. NEW-YORK. NO. 11.

"Dans le siècle où nous sommes
On ne donne rien pour rien."—MOLIERE.

GIL BLAS, before he was more than a day's journey away from Oviedo, fell in with a very common sort of personage, who wore a long rapier and a ready tongue; and who was so lavish of his praises as to win the best half of the traveler's omelette and a capital trout to his supper. I am inclined to think our town public not very unlike the thriving hero of Le Sage; and that a stranger cannot ordinarily hit upon a better method of winning his suppers, or an omelette, than by rankly dubbing our city an 'Eighth wonder of the world.' But the truth is, that between sarsaparillas, pills, lectures, and new books, the town is so cram full of puffery and praises, that I have not thought it worth my while to follow in the same track of senseless encomium. It has become even more vulgar than it was on the lips of the toady of Peñaflor: and from having been a tribute paid by the world on days of dividend, it has become a part of the small coin of social interchange: as Swift says, 'the trouble of collecting it from the world was too great, and the moderns have, therefore, bought out the *fee-simple.*'

Thus, though I may have lost my suppers of trout, and present favor, I trust that I may come in by-and-by for a little moderate good-will, and like Burchell, in the Vicar of Wakefield, who said 'fudge' at all the talk in the Primrose family, I shall hope at the end to be credited a disinterested purpose, and win a more thorough regard than any of the young Squire Thornhills, who are so lavish of their compliments, but who use them only to seduce innocence, or to feed an overweening vanity. The reader will remember, too, that the enthusiasm of the old visitor at the Vicar's frequently led him into harshness of expression, of which the sting was only removed when it was found, on longer acquaintance, that his love of honesty, and detestation of all manner of chicane, was but the prompter to his severity. May I not hope likewise, notwithstanding my neglect of praise, a little of that return which in the end made glad the philanthropic Burchell?

It is by no means from lack of subject that I have foresworn praises; indeed, they abound. Leaving private life, and the gayety of our salons, where enough of modesty, of womanly refinement, and delicacy are still exhibited, to counterbalance the persiflage of ignorant intruders, and the boldness of such as make unmaidenly display their object,—I might turn to the chapter of the public charities, and show you a whole town earnest to assist, in their distresses, those poor families who but a little while ago were so cruelly shattered by the wreck in Hague street. I might point to a score of monuments of both public and private munificence; I might note the open cordiality with which the stranger is received and welcomed: and the statesman, or benefactor, fêted and applauded. But of this there is no need: and even were it needful, I am utterly supplanted: the monopoly of such work has been long ago assigned over by common consent to occasional orators, speakers at public dinners, town journals, lady dancers, and Opera managers.

It is, indeed, not a little odious, and sometimes

painful, to find myself almost alone, if not worse than alone, among those who represent the harsher aspects of the town-life, its unmeaning parade, and its senseless, social habitudes: but I console myself with the reflection that not a few, and those worthy of most devoted regard, will see underlying all the irony and animadversion, enough of an honest purpose and a true humanity, to redeem my character. Were it not so, Fritz, I would long ago have thrown down my pen in despair, and looked as idly as the idlest upon the shifting currents of our town-life.

COUNTRY STRANGERS.

"Nor would I, you should melt away yourself
In flashing bravery, lest while you affect
To make a blaze of gentry to the world,
A little puff of scorn extinguish it.
I'd ha you sober, and contain yourself,
Not that the sail be bigger than the boat."
EVERY MAN IN HIS HUMOR. Act 1, Sc. 1.

I HAVE already given you a glimpse of the Bostonian, but he is not the only one among the strangers in our town who is deserving of particular mention. The Philadelphian is apt to fancy himself every whit as good as the Bostonian, and much better than the New Yorker. He prides himself overmuch upon the cut of his clothes, and until within a few years it was currently understood that the tailor craft in the Quaker city, was vastly superior to anything this side of the French capital; but I very much fear that they are losing ground in this particular, and can now no more compare their heroes of the needle with our Piercie Shaftons, than their Fairmount with the Croton, or Laurel Hill with Greenwood. Still, the Philadelphian has his claims to superiority; and though he does not boast now of a United States Bank, or Nicholas Biddle, he makes up by talk about the Girard College and Liberty Hall: he is eminently fond of the fancied European aspect of his streets: and whoever has talked with a stray Philadelphian without hearing somewhat of the charms of Chestnut street, must needs have been 'hard of hearing.' At dinner he is not a little disposed to speak modestly of the treasures of his market—its poultry, fruit, and eggs; nor does the Philadelphia lady once admit that our haberdashers display anything like so tasty a stock, as may be found at Levy's.

The Philadelphian enjoys, moreover, the consideration—though he forbears to urge it, and though he lives in the city of brotherly love—of belonging to a population capable of more mob enthusiasm, than any out of sight of the hills which overtop Lyons upon the Rhone. Following upon this quality, though how intimately associated with it I do not know, is his boast of the superior culture in Philadelphia society: and one might safely imagine from his conversation—using it in way of testimony, and not as sample—that the erudition and polish of a Philadelphia salon was something very hard to be found, beyond the sound of the trickle of Fairmount.

He would make it appear that money has little chance in his city, against the predominating influence of refinement and breeding; and he will point out to you our grocer's daughter swimming through the mazes of the waltz in the top circles of the town, as an impropriety that would quite shock the sensibilities of the tonnish ladies upon the Schuylkill. I find, however, that like the phlegmatic Bostonian, he is not insensible to the graces of such parvenus; and that, whether amorous of the money, or the figure, he is quite content to carry her off to his city, hush up her origin, and engraft upon her humble stock the elegancies of his elevated life. Of course, she thus loses every vulgar taint, and like the knotted dwarf stocks, on which the Burlington gardeners set their Flemish scions, is quite lost under the luxuriant foliage of the new growth.

The Philadelphians are adepts in whatever relates to hair-dye, gloves, or perfumery; and you will be able in four instances out of five to detect the visitor from that city, either by the dressing of his hair, the color of his gloves, or the scent of his trail. You will find his locks most skillfully laid apart, and rounded up over his ears as daintily as on the wig-blocks in Chestnut street; while one of our New York clubmen shall show in his back-hair, such a bristly and agonized parting, as would shock the worst bred North country buck, in the Assize-room of York.

The Philadelphian, too, cultivates a gentleness and softness of manner, which proves quite taking with our romantic school-girls; and singular as it may seem, he will preserve this softness and delicacy up to an advanced age: even the lawyers are fond of genteel pleas, and the doctors, though given marvelously to blood-letting, practice with the softest handling, on the softest pulses in the world.

The Washingtonian sometimes wanders to our city, though never unmindful of his majestic Potomac, and magnificent Capitol. He contrasts, much to our loss, the unpretending Broadway with the *sweep** of his Pennsylvania Avenue. There is

* Those who have seen Washington under a high wind in dry weather will see a reason in the italics; those who have not, will please restore the Roman character, and pass on.

no great peculiarity to distinguish him, unless it be a certain careless independence, as if he were, by virtue of his position, a supervisor of the nation. His dress and manner are of a mixed sort, being picked up from such vagabond tailors and hair-dressers as have taken refuge in the District—set off with careless imitation of Sir Henry Bulwer's hat or whiskers, and an assumption of the pretty off-hand airs of an Ambassador's Clerk.

The ladies would be even less distinguishable, were it not for an extraordinary air of boldness, which thrives excellently well in our Metropolis. For dress, they adopt with no little tact, such fashions of the New York or Philadelphia beauties as suit their style ; and for self-possession, and readiness of speech, I think they may be safely matched against any lady that smiles. Indeed, I do not know a better cure for maidenly diffidence—not that it is a common failing in our town—than a two months' residence at Washington.

From time to time, a Member who has decamped, may be seen in our streets, wearing in an important way the honors of his position ; and looking out upon our city as only one among his numerous constituencies. He is, perhaps, a little surprised that his appearance does not create a stir ; more especially as his arrival has been announced in the Express, and if a slave-holder—possibly in the Herald. It is matter very likely of some astonishment that the dinner invitations do not flow in upon him by dozens; and that the street-passers are so very ignorant as they appear to be, of what manner of man is among them. Nor will the Member cut a much more important figure in the ball-room, than in the street. In the dance, which he cannot in New York as in Washington avoid, he will find his stiff ungainliness no match for the little pliant fellows who are fresh from their Saracco lessons; and his political talk and careless toilette will be speedily thrust in a corner, or silenced with the sop of *ècarté*. Let him win fame, or fight a duel, and he shall dance 'fit for a Duke;' and he shall kiss in public or private, by proxy or otherwise, half the ladies of the town.

Some limbs of the army or navy, will from time to time excite quite a furor among our street-walkers, and will carry a flippant, assured manner that puts them entirely out of the reach of ordinary civilians. They are said, however, to be respectable, harmless fellows in their way, and quite comfortable companions at a supper, or a quiet rubber of whist.

Here and there about the hotels, you will see gentlemen of very important aspect, who cannot conceal their surprise, that everybody is not taking note of their bigness; whereas very few, not even the head porter or newspaper boys, are aware of their importance. They are the judges, or great men of country towns, excessively admired and honored in their own parish, renting the most conspicuous pew in their country church, and possibly keeping the best gig and brown mare in the whole township. Probably they have little properties, which pass with their humble neighbors as 'estates;' but they do not figure largely in our town. It does not occur to their embarrassed perceptions, that amid a population of half a million, all bent on their own affairs, the chances of the great man of a small town, for making a stir by his entrée, are, to say the least, very problematical. He should not take it too much to heart, if the passers-by do not dock their hats to him, or if his name is omitted from the personal movements of the Express.

I really entertain serious pity for such misguided gentlemen;—most of all at table, where their loud tones, dignified carriage, and patronizing looks thrown to their opposite neighbors, would seem to merit a larger share of consideration than they ever receive. But I am consoled with believing that, if not admired, their own sense of dignity does not at all flag; and they are sustained by a self-approval that is never at fault, and never weary of working.

Stout youngsters, too, from western cities, perhaps making first purchases on their own account, are quite disposed to carry off a good many of the street honors of the town; and have evidently prevailed on themselves to believe, that their appearance at the Opera may create quite a sensation: it will be perhaps true of their coat, or carriage, but for the rest they will be doomed in most instances to severe disappointment. Some individual of decided western habit and dress, who has imbibed to the full that pseudo American independence, which mocks at all forms, and even glories in pertness and singularity, will stare about him complacently, as if he were as capable of the highest art, as of making a stump speech in central Ohio. And he smokes his cigar, and wears his hat with very much the air of that Scotch traveler in Switzerland, of whom Goldsmith speaks:—he had wandered into a church where all the people were afflicted with goitres: they of course stared at his slim neck prodigiously: 'I perceive,' said he, rising to retire, 'that I am an odd fellow here, but I assure you that I am considered a good-looking man at home.'

I must not forget, Fritz, to give you a portrait or

two of our stranger ladies. An American lady is not without pride: and if it would not be counted ungallant, I should say she had more of it, than any woman in the world beside. Not a few, whom we may call country fashionables, and who make semi-annual pilgrimages to the shrine of Mr. Stewart, are exceedingly anxious to be mistaken for New Yorkers; and are curiously apprehensive lest any action, or wry adjustment of dress should make their provincial character perceptible. They are mightily observant of dress and gait; and if they find their country Pythoness has imposed upon them a mantilla, or hat, the like of which is not to be seen, they will be sure to carry back with them a little stock of upbraiding

Such lady is apt to run to the very verge of fashion, in her anxiety to meet the demands of provincial taste, which is somewhat spasmodic in its manifestations: and she must be well assured that the lawyer's, or apothecary's wife of her town, will not outshine her in finery. She is anxious to conceal any little innocent *gaucherie* that may pertain to her, even from the clerks of the trading establishments; and will assume an easy familiarity with them, and counterfeit an acquaintance with goods, and store-keeping generally, that is quite refreshing to look upon. Nor is she ever ignorant of anything, which in her view a city lady ought to know: and she cultivates an *abandon*, of a caste rarely to be met with out of the public parlors of the hotels.

Her conversation is not demure or quiet, but lively: and she not unfrequently hums (if she knows it) a snatch of a fashionable Opera. If a friend calls, to ask when she came up to town, and how all the 'folks' are in Jersey, she blinks him with very few words; she turns talk as speedily as possible upon the Opera, and the town topics, and chats in the glibest possible style of Mesdames So-and-so, of the spring modes, and fashionable books. She has no idea of being beaten off into provincial topics in public places. At the Opera, she wears the air of one who is not in the least taken aback by whatever she may see, and as if she understood the gist of the whole matter, as well as the keenest of the critics.

Opposed to these in their action, are the timid, modest ladies from the country, who have not known enough of the city to be baited by its assumptions; they *dress* innocently for breakfast, and you will meet them at nine in the morning in brilliant evening attire. Yet withal they are very fearful that people are looking at them, and very certain that their dress is a very pretty one. They

26

are sometimes betrayed in their naïveté into looking through a shop-window, and blush to find themselves surrounded by such ungenteel people.

They labor under almost constant alarm about their purses ; and from the stories they have heard, are disposed to reckon nearly every over-dressed man either a pickpocket or cut-throat. In this they are not far from right : still, in broad daylight, upon Broadway, they may consider themselves comparatively safe.

They are afraid of theatres ; and if from New England, the fear is accompanied with very zealous and decided condemnation. The Museum does not of course come under the same category, and may be ventured on in virtue of an old moral tradition, by all those who are too good for the Opera or Niblo's. If the mother of a family, our good lady will be very fearful, on her first visits, of the contamination of her boys ; and will look suspiciously upon every sour, or moustached face, she sees upon the street. She will mistake even the most common acts of politeness, for the seductive arts of unprincipled and designing men.

She is subject to unceasing, and most unnecessary alarms at sight of any street-gathering, and is convinced there must be a pickpocket or murderer in the case; she is afraid of the cabmen, lest she be cheated or hurried off out of the reach of humanity, and be lost to herself, her family, and the world. Of the omnibus drivers, she has but little better opinion, and an absolute certainty that a pick-pocket is in every stage. She wears her vail down in passing the Hospital, that she may not become infected with any town cholera : and is in a distressing panic at sight of an engine, or at the cry of fire.

Yet withal, Fritz, these very good women of the country, who are the butts of city ridicule, will in nine cases out of ten, rear sons who will take the lead away, in business, in professional pursuits, or in the arts, from the most luxurious of the town-bred. They will prove the efficient and active movers of our vast body politic, while the sons of millionaires are contenting themselves with the empty town distinctions of a dashing coat, or a tawdry epaulette. Town worthies, who with their brilliant social strides, entered upon while yet only half through their grammars, are thinking to outstrip, and throw into ludicrous insignificance, the slowly accumulating manhood of provincial youths, will find realized, to their mortification, the old fable of the hare and the tortoise. Steady effort, persevering industry, and right moral teaching, is even now in obscure corners, laying the basis of characters, which twenty years hence, will control the wealth, and the public interests of the town.

Dress, equipages, perfumery, and the Opera will always have native, city teachers; but the Pulpit, the Exchange, Journalism, and the Bar, are drawing in recruits from the rough sons of hard country study, and of old-fashioned, rigid, academical education, whose energy, spirit, and influence, will one day make the hot-house progeny of the town quiver in their shoes.

Show me an influential journalist, a rising man at our bar, a preacher at once profound and practical, a physician eminent in his profession, a merchant who is fertile in enterprise, and successful by honest industry, and I will show you one who knew little or nothing of the fashionable life of the town, until his mental and moral character was already formed. On the other hand, show me a lawyer rich in political intrigue, a doctor distinguished by nostrums, a conversationalist fertile in equivoques, a poetaster fatiguing the language with his poverty, a merchant who is rich by successive bankruptcies, or defalcations, and twenty to one, he has been dandled in the endearing arms of Fashion, and while yet in his teens, has converted his feeble art of the grammar, to the crowning arts of the boudoir.

FAMILY AND ANCESTORS

"—— jamás te pongas á disputar de linages, á lo menos comparándolos entre si, pues por fuerza en los que se comparan, uno ha de ser el mejor, y del que abatieres serás aborrecido, y del que levantares en ninguna manera premiado."—DON QUIXOTE, Part II. Cap. XLIII.

THIS is a tender subject, my dear Fritz; and it is capital advice that the old Don gives his Squire: little may be gained in broaching it, and much may be lost. But my notices of the town-life would be sadly incomplete, if I were to omit the consideration of so important an element in the graduation of our social scale.

The pride which inauces a man to cherish the memory of an honored, and respected ancestor, is not an ignoble pride,—nor is it an unusual one; and he must be a sot indeed who is insensible to the regard, which by common acclaim should attach to the name of his sire. But this ancestral pride needs some caution in the using; it may serve as the groundwork of very dangerous boastings, and attract a degree of attention, or provoke a contrast, that the boaster can very poorly bear. A simpleton who should forever be declaiming upon the talent of an ancestor, would only make his weakness the more palpable, and draw down the reproach of having harmed a great name, by association with a pitiful soul. As he cannot be great himself, it were much better that he did not trace his descent from greatness.

Yet strange as it may seem, Fritz, these are the very ones who are forever talking of their pedigree, and raking up from their family tombs, a distinction which could never belong to their family character. Nothing indeed is more natural than for the man, who has not within himself the means of challenging popular esteem, to take it boldly from the ashes of his fathers: necessity, in a measure, justifies the action, and the theft of the bread of ancestral distinction, is pardonable in those descendants, who are starving under the hunger of contempt.

You may think, Fritz, that such observations have no aptness in my studies of this Republican town; but if so, you would be strangely mistaken. Our Republicanism has not yet so far individualized the man or the family, as to make either reliant solely on their own action, name, or character, for distinction.

We have not only the old and meritorious pride in family names, honorably associated with our Colonial History, but the importation of other foreign luxuries has brought in its train, an immense amount of the worship of family splendor and imaginary genealogies; which as they make the basis of much of the feudal aristocracy, are serving as the apologies and adornments of our own. They are just the apologies indeed, which are needed to make it good, and render it effective among those whom it is intended to impress.

A man's own distinction and successes are losing their force amid the classified and billeted brilliants of our upper circles. The homely honor of having wrought out a name for one's self, or of having accumulated, by successful and public spirited enterprise, a great estate, is beginning to lose ground before that spirit of conventionality and foreign imitativeness, which finds its best types in liveries, spurious heraldry, or in the habit of display and of exclusion.

Our rising men, of such callings as have heretofore been reckoned outcast, are beginning to understand this matter, and are learning that bravado, and well-cut coats-of-arms are better worth, than any study of refinement, or pretence for cultivation. Families of our town will presently be known from their crests, and all our brokers make their serving-men conspicuous by a vulture stamped upon their buttons. The Digg's livery, and the Mugg's coach will be the best descriptive types of the respective families, and will be as familiarly known as the coat-collar of Northumberland, or the hat-band of the Marquis of Westminster. All this serves as the mark of a distinction, which might otherwise escape notice, and secures to the offspring, a comfortable ancestral basis, without any fees at the herald's office.

But we are not yet so far gone in European notions, nor so blinded by these miserable excuses and cravings for title, but that their flimsiness is sometimes seen through distinctly enough, to expose the wretched poverty of what is behind. Imagine an honest and respectable grocer, tailor, shopkeeper, or whomever you please, not showing any pride in that industry which has wrought out for him an independence, nor making his tastes and expenditures keep cheerful and honored company, but like a scurvy coward that he is, turning his back on the trade that has enriched him, and trying to hide its remembrance by new-vamped crests, and the blazonry of a coach panel! What sort of manly republican independence is this? Let him trick himself as he will, the peacocks, whose plumes he has stolen, will have their peck at him, and the sable jackdaws, to whose tribe he belongs, will utterly despise him!

Observe, Fritz, that I am throwing out no sneers upon any particular calling or trade. It would ill become me, a pamphleteer, without name (and as my honored friend, Mrs. K——, alledges, 'not in society '*), to be so bold. Why should we, indeed, in any manner decry, or make light of those envied *possibilities* which our blessed Republic guaranties, and which will make the coal-boy of to-day, the judge, or the millionaire of to-morrow? There is no trade, and no profession, which is not respectable for an American, except the trade of pretence, and the trade of dishonesty.

And it is this very pretence, my dear Fritz, that I want most to rebuke; it is the covering up of the individual, and his personal acts or acquisitions, with the patched and parti-colored coat of an adopted European artificiality; it is the shame for what we are, and the pretension to what we are not. That American must be weak indeed, who wishes to prop up his republican manhood on the rotten stilts of an extinct feudalism! I will not envy him if he stands, nor pity him if he falls.

My up-stairs neighbor, the gray-haired lodger, with whom I have had frequent conversations on this, as well as kindred topics, considers himself, by virtue of a name bearing the Dutch prefix of Van, one of the 'old families;' and though he is as

* In this matter, I am content to throw myself with pride upon my own *incognito*, and to stake the battered head of the LORGNETTE at the top of my sheet, against all the escutcheons, tinctures, and charges of an hermaphrodite heraldry.

poor as a Christian need be, he yet looks with ineffable disdain upon what he calls the pretenders of the day. His name, and a snuff-box, are all that have come down to him from a glorious ancestry. He cherishes both with equal pride and tenderness, and never taps at his box without thanking Heaven that he was born a Van.

He of course reckons the broad-skirted Dutchmen as the elder members of our aristocracy, and is disposed to look with strong sentiments of distrust upon any which does not smack of the old Dutch flavor. He affects great indifference at sight of the equipages and houses of our up-town great, and talks complacently of the time when our neighborhood was the centre of wealth and respectability. Indeed, he humors his fancy with the idea that a large proportion of it still remains, though I must confess that we have but a scurvy set of neighbors. I am strongly inclined to think that the old gentleman, with all his pride, would be tempted to give up his broad skirts, and the Van to his name, if he could only secure a good slice each day from the comfortable dinners that our parvenus are consuming; for the love of the luxury that wealth brings, is, I find, a most prevalent affection, as well of old families, as of new ones; and nothing will so reconcile most men to lack of ancestral badges, and a sounding name, as a plentiful provision of all the comforts of life, and a free license to indulge.

Among the pleasant little artifices which are adopted by those emulous of ancestral honors, is that of changing the name, by transposition of a letter or two, into something having strong affinities with the great names of history : this practice, if followed up with philologic attention, will result before many generations, in an entire transformation, and in the open possession of an ancestral root and tree, that will most amply repay the pains-taking. A change of pronunciation, if insisted on, will not unfrequently do wonders, in giving an air to a man's title ; and if sufficiently romantic, or illustrious, it may serve to christen a country-seat, or a town residence—much to the undisguised admiration of the suburban classes.

Wealth of itself, is not understood to create any immediate ancestral claims ; time enough must elapse for the life and death of an hypothecated ancestry ; which time has been shortened down in some instances to the very brief period of three or four winters. A short period, it is true, as the world goes generally ; but we 'manage those things better in our town.'

I do not mean to say, Fritz, that wealth supposes

no ancestry at all, which to be sure, would leave a frightful hiatus for modesty to tumble in; but it is such as is not suited to the boasts of the heir; and might possibly be as irksome to his pride as that hinted at in the French couplet:

> "Comment s'appelait ton père ?
> C'est le secret de ma mêre."

What particular action, or claims upon distinction, are of the best complexion to make up a good, compact, ancestral reputation, I can hardly tell. Services rendered the state would of course weigh considerably; but if I might be permitted to judge from existing examples, I should say that the accomplishment of nothing, either for the state or the town, was nearly as good. Be as it may, however, distinguished families are multiplying like witchcraft. New families are dying out, and old ones are sprouting all over the town. They will presently become as plentiful as they are in Virginia.

You have heard, Fritz, Southey's bad story of the New Gate Calendar—how it was bought up by American Colonists, looking up their genealogies. If the Messrs. Harper would undertake a reprint, and the Tribune and Courier give their favorable notices, we have no doubt but it would prove a profitable venture.

I have often wondered, my dear Fritz, what a

curious figure the ancestors of our ladies and gentlemen of ton would cut, if suffered to come up to the light, and mingle for a little time in the festivities of the town. Not that they would be cordially welcomed by all their distinguished issue, for we fancy that many a poor knight of the needle, or awl, would be shuffled off very unceremoniously and very unfilially, into the basement rooms.

In one quarter we should see a broad-skirted old Dutchman, in cocked hat, and with cane mounted with buck-horn, wheezing and puffing down some dim business alley in search of his great-grandson, or perhaps coming upon him in his dancing practice, and uttering an indignant 'Dunder and Blixem,' at the unscrupulous familiarity of the Saracco women. In another direction we might find some great expounder of colonial jurisprudence, searching out his descendants among the newly rich, emulous of rivaling the show of their neighbors, and not at all, of sustaining the intellectual dignity of the name. A humble, dapper little fellow, of a century back, familiar in his day with shears or yard-stick, and who had left a company of dapper girls comfortably at the counter, would burst upon his great-grandchildren amid all the brilliancy of the Opera, and watch with wondering eyes at their well-modulated applause of such music as he surely never heard before death,—and it would be uncharitable to suppose he had heard such since.

Some rusty old coachman might resume his place upon the box of a carriage, in which the pink of our fashion, his posterity, are rustling in silks; and many a grandpapa would, if invited filially to the home of his descendants, whet an appetite with French ragouts, that in the old reign of the flesh had sated itself on cheese and Dutch herring.

But quite the worst of it all would be, that the poor ancestry would be wished heartily back to the hottest of places, rather than have their insignificance, and real presence, mar the lustre of our 'old families.' There would be such bitter tears shed over their reappearance, as never watered their funeral or tombs; and the unoffending little cobblers would be hurried off to their leather and lapstone, as peremptorily as when old Peter Stuyvesant caught them at their political meddling.

Yet this revival, Fritz, of the true state and pomp of our ancestry would be a most republican display:—great because of its diversity, and of the proof it would offer of that social elasticity, which belongs to our scheme, and which will ensure to industry and integrity, whatever may be its station, wealth and honor. Alas, for human nature, that it should blush for its necessities, and that such effort should be made to hide an origin, which is perhaps the only basis of its honor!

And in this connection, my dear Fritz, I cannot forbear turning my glass toward that painful tragedy whose blood and mystery have not yet passed from the minds of men. I allude to a recent murder, which may be traced back, step by step, to the impulses of a social pride; a desire to blend, and be even with that assumed and admitted aristocracy, which, though it might have been based on refinement, needed, in the judgment of the unfortunate culprit, the trappings of wealth for its sustenance.

If social education and popular habit had not grafted upon him the inevitable necessity of doing something more than regular performance of duty, and basing his position upon something more showy than gentlemanly address, the motive would have been wanting to those first oversteppings of the means of living, to that obliquity which induced unfairness of commercial dealing, and to the final issue of the dreadful tragedy. Dr. Webster (if guilty) is as much the victim of our social heresies, as he is of a brutal passion. If men had been respected more entirely for what *they* are, and not for what their habitations or their dinners are, Dr. Webster might still have been the respectable lecturer, the successful subduer of his own passions, and the esteemed father. But the obeisance paid to wealth and to genteel living, was strong enough and general enough to bear him down in its tide; and in the fear of being submerged, he must needs thrust another under—to the grave.

It is idle to say that he would have been as much respected, if his living had been modest and commensurate with his means; probably he might have been; but the popularity and commonness of an opposing opinion, making its manifestations most strong and patent, seduced him from such belief—to his fall.

Not one bankruptcy in five but owes its origin to the same social causes; and the 'getting into society' with curtains and coaches, is a fallacy that is 'getting' a great many very fast out of the bounds of honesty and independence.

Nor will I forbear, Fritz, to enter my testimony with pride, to the dignity of that Court which has not been shaken by prominence of social position, and which has weighed talent and scientific attainment as nothing, when opposed to those great interests of humanity and common justice which our Republican rule professes to protect.

TIMON.

APRIL 24. NEW-YORK. NO. 12.

Quid scribam, vobis, *Lectores*, aut quomodo scribam, aut quid omninò non scribam; Dii me Deæque (*homines feminæque*) pejus perdant quàm perire quotidie sentio.—Tacit. (*ad* Timonis *fidem emendatus*.)

The sick Tiberius was never at more loss to know in what humor he should address the Roman Senate, than I to discover what topic will best suit my town-readers. Not a few have suggested that I give further sketches of the Opera, with dainty episodes upon the extravagances of dress, and inuendoes which would touch here and there along the range of boxes. I have been advised that such and such persons, by virtue of some moral obliquity, were fair game, and that the scandal of the exhibition, if ornamented with the quiet simplicity of my narrative, would add hugely to the name and repute of my work. One is represented as having forgotten the duties of a wife, and even the moral dignity of a mother. Another, it is said, has by common assent, perverted all her womanly delicacy; and by a series of eccentricities, which as John Tyler would say, are 'conterminous' with immorality, has rendered herself the fair, and deserving target of all a penman's arrows. But if kind advisers would allow me, Vice is not always to be determined by its most palpable exhibition: and John Timon, in the course of his life, has seen enough to show that Virtue may sometimes lie hidden under the idiosyncrasies of native wanton, and that all the sanctiomonious airs of a vestryman, or a deacon, may cover the lusts that spring from the devil.

Another most goodly patron has suggested to my publisher, that the church quarrels, which, unfortunately, are not rare, would offer capital topic for what they were pleased to call, the flowing periods of Timon. And very many who have little to boast of, except a hankering after scandal, have urged upon me the adoption of something more of personality and directness of issue; and have covered up their cravings under the softly charge, that my papers were 'too gentlemanly.'

Is it not sadning, my dear Fritz, to believe that the town-taste is so set on edge with the vinegar of such as push their writings to the furthest edge of delicacy, that no modest and subdued discourse upon the social habits of the day, can be received with any relish whatever? Where, in the name of Heaven, are we running, when modesty must hide its face, and when the gross scandal of a divorce trial, or the brûtal developments of our city police, make up the entertainment of those who read, and of those who guide our tâste? Answer me, Fritz,—is popularity worth enough that a man should fling behind him social proprieties, and fraternize with the lewd panders to our growing appetite for scandal and immodesty?

Must I, to make my letters 'taking,' abandon the better impulses which belong to me as a plain country gentleman,—duck to the habit of the town, and offend against those proprieties, by which alone I know how to set valuation on society?

I know, Fritz, that I lose much by forbearance; when the personalities of scurrilous paragraphists are read with unction, how can a simple talker about pöpular extravagances be listened to with any degree of attention? They who have surfeited their appetites on leeks and onions, will surely turn up their noses at the mustard and oil of even a well-dressed salad.

Indeed, were I to attempt to give to my papers what my good critics would call the spice of personal invective, it would require far more art than I am possessed of, to steer adroitly between the host of conflicting social jealousies, and to be sure of winning kind consideration of one party, by hearty abuse of another. Madame Dolittle might be intensely gratified if I were to give the public a tricksy portraiture of her rival, but most kind friend, the Dowager Nettleton; and the interesting Miss Squibbs would very likely laugh incontinently at any sketch of what she reckons the improprieties, or the genteel pretensions of her pretty neighbors. Those whose moderate intelligence serves as a sort of bar to any literary reunions, would thank me kindly for painting some rubicund young lady declaiming before a select circle, her own sonnets, or a page of Mr. Tupper; and Miss Homely would be delighted at my exhibition of some scandalous expôse of her pretty friend, in a private tableau. People who make up their virtue out of a plain carriage, and their religion out of two sermons a week, would bid me, perhaps, God-speed, in reproducing the heraldry of their coach-driving friends, and in puncturing the windy morality which is blown up by pretty-mouthed preachers, and guarded by imposing ceremonial.

The small critics who give proof of head and tongue by overmuch snarling, and who draw public attention by their yelps at the heels of the great, would very likely give me an encouraging snuffle, if I were to join them in their canine pursuits; and all the women of pliable virtue would honor me with abundance of smiles, if I were to attempt detraction of the pure and high-minded.

But while thinking to gain ground, I might be inadvertently a great loser; and scratch deep, where I only thought to curry favor. Prudence, as well as propriety, forbids then, my dear Fritz, that I should enter upon any invidious, personal strictures; those who love such topic are referred to the sources which are kindred with their tastes; they will find none of it here; my mask shall not be abused for any stealthy strokes; and whoever worries his vanity with the thought of personal injury, shall, upon due authentication of his griefs, find a man to answer him.

But in virtue of those kind friends who are so tenderly solicitous that a little more of the caustic should be applied, and who are plainly of opinion that personal sketches would derogate in no degree from the character for propriety, which my paper sustains, I have determined to note down their names; and whenever, in the aggregate, they shall present such a pretty range of characteristics as to tempt my pen, they shall be honored with particular attention: and thus, modestly, and without intention, they will become the heroes and heroines of their own suggestion. A half dozen such are already on my list, but thus far I am compelled to say, that their vanities are so small, and their vices of so common-place a character, that they will not avail to point a period, even with the most dexterous of handling. But let them not live without hope; common-places are sometimes remarkable by aggregation, and even *niasérie* has its heroes.

AUTHORS AND AUTHORLINGS.

'He who would shun criticism, must not be a scribbler; and he who would court it, must have great abilities, or great folly.'—MONRO.

'Good authors damned have their revenge in this,
—To see what wretches gain the praise they miss.'—YOUNG.

I HAVE said, Fritz, that modesty would belong to my remarks on literary men, or matters; but what reviewer, from Mr. Brownson to Dr. Griswold, was ever modest? It is a quality that does not belong to the craft ; and the moment that my pen touches paper, to give you some of the characteristics of our literary men, all my efforts to sustain a proper degree of humility vanish most strangely. But if all sense of modesty is lost, I shall be at least kept in countenance by the herd of town critics, not one of whom but thinks himself as capable of analyzing the most abstruse theory in metaphysics, as of dividing into stops the full chorus of the Opera.

Should I so far forget myself, as to speak of the works of town-writers with an air of levity, and a tone of judgment which would seem to bespeak a higher power, and a finer eye in the critic, than in the author, let the audacity be credited where it properly belongs—to a slight infection with the critical rabies, and not to the impertinence of a humble country gentleman. It is possible that a little lurking desire to gratify my vanity impels me ; for there is scarcely a better way that a vain man can take, to raise himself to a fair literary level, than by so lowering the platform on which stand the literary tribe, as to make his humble position less apparent. Nor is this pulling down of the platform, effected as I find, so much by open abuse, as by a wonderfully nice critical analysis, a few kind words, a happy familiarity of expression, and such other means as may go to show the critic fully capable of judging, and even rich enough to fling out a few tid-bits of praise.

Indeed, had I ambition for authorship, further than editing these occasional papers, I do not know how I could so well make a respectable name as by respectable abuse and praise of the living town-authors ; this would gain one credit with the publishing craft, and would ensure abundance of applications to edit the works of dead writers, and to write prefaces to the works of the new-born. Moreover, I should be very sure of purchase at the hands of the authors themselves, (and this would make no inconsiderable sale,) who are as crazily anxious to know what is said of them, as a woman of doubtful position. I could count safely, too, on the praises of all the authors I had seemed to commend, and on the hearty abuse of the rest. Better aids than these to a 'town run' could hardly be desired.

Our book-reading world has, I find, its periodic fevers of literary fancy, a sort of author cholera-morbus, which leaves the public mind in a very debilitated condition ; nor does it operate much more favorably upon the writer ; since it reduces him in most instances to a state of sad depletion, if not of decided collapse.

As illustrative of this, you will remember, I

think, Fritz, a furor which some years ago attended the publication of a book called 'The Glory and the Shame of England,' but which so completely exhausted itself by excess of effusion, that a biography of Sam. Houston, and the rich elaboration of a most extraordinary 'Ivory Cross,' could not wholly revive it. The 'Gallery of distinguished Americans,' with fairly done lithographs, in lieu of engravings, will make a better hit, it is to be hoped, than the discharge upon the Texan President;—as much more effective, in short, as a revolver than a single barrel. Our distinguished men will surely not be so ungrateful as to withhold some reasonable 'reward of merit.'

Again, not long since, about the period of the publication of 'Napoleon and his Marshals,' the public was sadly affected with a kind of battle and thunder delirium, which did not abate until after very much blood-letting, and a quieting dose of the Sacred and profane (Adirondack) Mountains. Those who were most sadly under the influence of the delirium, have endeavored to give the best possible evidence of recovery, by heaping inordinate, and most undeserved abuse upon the unfortunate author, who so little time ago, bewitched them with the force and vigor of his language. The name of this author has been occasionally associated by some over-shrewd ones with the LORGNETTE. It is surely not a little droll that suspicion of any martial propensities should attach to the rustic plainness of Timon; let the wiseacres pick me out, if they can, a musket, a general, or a Sinai, in the whole range of my papers.

The Tupper fever has become almost chronic, but it is not now in so active a state of eruption as a year or two since; its outbreak was attributed to an inoculation by Mr. Willis, through the medium of a little vaccine matter supplied by the Home Journal. It is now understood to be confined chiefly to school-girls, and literary young women. It was a remarkable symptom of this disorder that those afflicted with it were accustomed, in their moments of delirium, to confound Martin Farquhar Tupper with Solomon, an ancient king of the Jews; the proverbial philosophy was bound up by church bookbinders, and even now may be seen on the tables of some afflicted sufferers, lying between the Prayer Book, and the Psalms of David.

There was at one time serious danger of a Festus outbreak; but either from the length of Mr. Bailey's poem, or some other cause which has not come to light, the danger has gone by; and the naive advice of Satan, and his piquant colloquies with Mr. Festus Bailey, are confined to scattered private rehearsals. The truth is, Satanic colloquies are so frequent now-a-days that no one can make a joke of their novelty ; and though comparatively few barristers can talk to the devil as well as the barrister Bailey, yet they make up amply by familiarity, what they lack in elegance.

The Jane Eyre malady amounted to an epidemic, and has sustained its ground, notwithstanding all the efforts of the doctors, to this time. The authoress is rapidly accumulating a stock of enthusiasm on this side of the water, which, if it do not previously explode, will by and by secure her a suite of rooms at the Irving, a confectioner's image of the maniac wife, and a classic ode from the Brigadier Morris, about the Cyclop Fairfield, and the adorable Bronte !

The Typee disorder was a novel one, of uncertain character, until clearly defined and made cognizable by a London issue of the book of Mr. Melville. It attacked with peculiar virulence adventurous school-boys, and romantic young ladies who have an eye for nature. At one time, shortly after the publication of Mardi, the disorder assumed a threatening malignancy, and patients were given over in despair to the chrono-thermal and homœopathic treatment. Latterly, however, the types have changed, and Peregrine Pickle and Robinson Crusoe, are safe cures for Redburn and White Jacket.

A highly contagious literary disease broke out not long since upon the appearance of a book called the 'Lady Alice.' It was supposed at first, from the highly conscientious and Evangelical views entertained by its publishers, to be of a religious order, and not calculated to heat much blood out of the pale of the true Church. It was found, however, to produce almost a frenzy, which rapidly overleaped all ecclesiastical barriers, and crept into every denomination of readers and thinkers. The worthy publishers undoubtedly felt some twinges of conscience at their evangelical error, and made such atonement as was in their power, by the issue of a cheap edition.

A check which was for a time imposed upon it by the superveyors of the Church, was found only to 'scatter' the disorder, and produce a general eruption upon the literary surface of society. The exquisite moral teachings of the book were enforced by most happy example; and its religious character was at once picturesque and artistic. It offered pretty inside views of the highly advanced state of European society, and of the artless blending of nature, morals, and religious æsthetics. It offered tempting footing for a new step in our social progress; and while it will multiply worthily the number of crosses, oratories, and confessional boxes, it will undoubtedly refine, in a corresponding degree, the foolish rigidity of an old-fashioned, Bible morality.

Los Gringos, careless, slipshod, uneasy, yet with a swift, invigorating canter, was rather in the nature of a St. Vitus' dance, and could scarcely be considered anything more than a cutaneous affection. Under the warm treatment, and pleasantly sweetened, mucilaginous drinks of the Home Journal and De Trobriand's Revue, it will probably have no very serious effects.

A kind of African fever, accompanied with great debility, broke out on the appearance of Kaloolah; its types were not unlike the Typee affection, and will probably yield to the same treatment. The author has been credited, I understand, in some quarters, (much to my honor) with the editing of the Lorgnette; but I would advise him, as he values the integrity of those peculiar manifestations which have followed upon his practice, and more than all, as he cherishes his brilliant reputation for chivalrous adventure with the colored woman of Africa, to repel indignantly the charge.

St. Leger was spasmodic, but not so serious in its manifestations, as might have been expected by the reiterated warnings held out by the 'Knickerbocker' quarantine. As a book, St. Leger is remarkable for short sentences, short chapters, German names, and Greek extracts. Though it has not created a run of fever, it has peculiarities of type, and an individualism of character, which will be well worth a report in the next annual account of our Dunglinson of literature—Dr. Griswold.

There are beside, a multitude of authors, whose works, so far from breeding any sudden epidemic, are most sedative in their operations; such writers are nice to an exception, and are respectable almost to a virtue. Their influence may be likened (to carry out our medical typography) to a mild influenza, characterized by frequent sneezings, to which old ladies are peculiarly subject, and easily curable by a little hot catmint, or a blue stocking applied to the neck.

Among these authors, Mr. T——n may be said to hold a place of proud eminence. Others would fairly escape notice, and the symptoms which follow upon their attack, would scarce be cognizable, without the acute discernment of that highly respectable literary practitioner, Dr. Griswold. He can be cordially commended to the humbler members of the literary profession, as a safe observer, and one whose faculty of auscultation is most minute. Would you believe it, my dear Fritz, that such laurels have been pinned to my ears, as the association of my papers with this Coryphæus of letters! I blush to find myself in the enviable light; and to have become by the mere accident of suspicion, the cynosure of admiring eyes!

The Willis affection is decidedly organic; and the varieties in its manifestation, have been as inconsiderable, as the changes in the types of the infecting matter. Thus we have had Pencillings, Inklings, Dashes, Glimpses, Ruralities, and People I have Met, all pleasantly running together; and any given quantity of which needs only the spice of a prefatory chapter, and a variation upon his most pliant name, to have the periodic run of a fashionable fever. It is surely no little commendation of an author, when by mere change of plate, or dressing, the public will devour his old dishes with as much *gout*, as the freshest meats of the new writers. How his matter will be served up next, and whether under imprimatur of N. P. W., or N. P. Willis, or N. Parker Willis, it would be quite unsafe to predict. Indeed, Mr. W.'s supple art of words renders it impossible to hazard any guess whatever; and I should not be greatly surprised if he were to change the name altogether, without at all destroying its integral character.

Mr. Willis has certainly amused and instructed,

in his way, a greater number of men, women, and children, within the last ten years, than almost any man on this side of the Atlantic; and his name is as familiar (I speak of the family name, and not the *titular* one) in cigar-shops and journalism, as it is in libraries, and the boudoir. How many of his readers he has improved in moral habit,—to how many he has given the pabulum for stirring and healthful thought, bracing up their nerves for hard work, and quickening them into honest endeavor, it would be very immodest in me to answer. How much he might have done, none can tell better than himself. Utility is surely not the prevailing characteristic of his writings; and he will hardly hope to be enrolled among the reformers of the age, whatever may become of his friends, Horace Greeley, Cornelius Matthews, or Dr. Griswold.

He is among the keenest of observers; and yet he might voyage through California, seeing nothing more than lack of ladies, and shabby toilettes; or he might make the north-west passage, and note only the icebergs and the northern lights. Yet not a better man could be found to bring away those minute observations of old countries which would go to show their social complexion, and the condition and habit of their civilization. After all, whatever particular qualities may be wanting, critical analysis cannot impair the individuality of his talent; and genius will be sure to leave a light in its wake, whichever way it may steer.

You will smile, Fritz, at the compliment, yet some wise ones have attributed our correspondence to this prince of paragraphists. Now, with due courtesy and modesty be it said, I cannot believe that the piquant leaders of the Home Journal, and the spice islands of his reading, would leave him margin enough, either of time or industry, to throw together the score of pages which light up each week your solitude. Nor can I find any trace of those prettily perplexed interchangements of phrase which are the charm of Home Journalists,—nor any of those light running similes which slide through his periods, like a sunbeam through a leafy thicket.

I am not conscious (and the public will acquit me) of any of those waving sinuosities of expression which belong to his language; and on which you are borne along—now up, now down,—like a boat floating over the swells of ocean. Here are none of those easy convolutions of words, which make the column of his type wind amid his subject-matter, like a Kaloolah serpent gliding through tropic foliage.

Mr. McCracken is a gentleman, who, though

not widely known to type, is by no means without his town admirers. A little disposition that belongs to him, to play Timon—not in the wood, but in the palace,—has called up his name in connection with my papers; and I am led to infer from all that can be learned, that the allegation should be accepted as a compliment. It costs very little to give compliments in the dark, as every plain woman knows; and while making due acknowledgments for the honor done me, I would at the same time caution those who are quite positive that the authorship lies in that quarter, (Judge B—— among the rest) against multiplying immoderately their wagers.

Mr. Carl Benson (Bristed) has come in for a share of the LORGNETTE honor; for which it is understood that his high classical attainments would amply qualify him and, indeed, entirely ensure the paper against any unfortunate errors of citation. You know, Fritz, that I make no scholarly pretensions, and that the trick of the pen is not old enough with me, to render my *lapsi pennæ* either unusual, or singular. Pray, Mr. B——, is it Seneca, who says,—

Nil sapientiæ odiosius acumine nimio?

With all gratitude to those who have attributed

my observations to the erudite, and irate antagonist of a distinguished professor, it is yet a source of regret, that even stray citations from classic authors, should have turned the current of suspicion toward a scholar, and so induced the belief with any, that these letters smack more of the closet than of the world. The public may return Mr. Benson to his special patronage of Catullus, and 'fast trotters,' and acquit him thoroughly of any inaccuracies which have crept into the letters of Timon.

Mr. R. G. White is a musical critic of the town, a gentleman, as I am informed, of fair taste, and considerable observation. Though not enrolled in the Griswold galaxy of authors, he will yet come under head of 'authorling,' and has been honored with a clay statuette. Though not over familiar with his works, yet I am content to take the verdict of the town-public in reckoning him a writer of shrewdness, tact, and elegance—the more especially, Fritz, since he is your reputed correspondent.

It would appear that he is an adept with an opera-glass, and should know much of the goings on in our brilliant town-world; at least so much of it as appears within the doors of the Opera-house. But he is, after all, I fancy, much too fond of his fiddle, and the composers, to have entered upon any such employment, as has been gratuitously assigned him.

Mr. Ik. Marvell (Mitchell) has also come in for a share of the suspicion; and although, perhaps, I ought to feel flattered by the association of my work with the name of either author or authorling, yet it does really seem that my unpretending, and straightforward sentences show very little to evidence the same paternity with the contortions and abruptnesses of the 'Battle Summer.' To say the least of it, my errors against grammar have not been willful; and my arrangement of style has not looked toward the quackery of dramatic effect.

Yet withal the compliment is acknowledged, since the same gentleman has written a most creditable book of travels, which of an idle hour, will repay a second reading. Mr. Marvell is certainly a promising young man, and with thus much of compliment, to sustain him for the loss, I relieve him entirely of the new and unnecessarily imposed burden of authorship.

Mr. Harry Franco (Briggs), a name not, perhaps, new to you, Fritz, has also been associated with our modest correspondence. He is said to possess a ready wit, and variety of attainment which would qualify him to do much better things than have appeared in the LORGNETTE. A little reflection of his honor was at one time, indeed, cast upon me by the Mirror newspaper: but latterly the penetrating editor of that journal finds my letters losing their 'Tom Peppery' character, and growing sadly stupid. Let the kind gentlemen bear with me; all philosophers cannot be Franklins: all restaurateurs cannot be Downings: and all authors cannot be Briggses.

Mr. Cornelius Matthews is another extraordinary member of the literary society of the town, upon whom has casually rested (I have it on his own authority) a share of those capricious suspicions, which Mr. Kernot's little weekly has created;—and this, notwithstanding his recent 'money-penny' labors. But on the other hand, it is objected, that no announcement of such implied authorship, or flattering paragraph, has appeared among the editorials of the Literary World. If John Timon had been Matthews, there would have been surely some trace of the heroic little Abel, if not allusion to the gallant Puffer Hopkins. A stouter Philippic, too, than I can by any possibility fish out of the inkstand, would have startled my readers into an international copyright frenzy, and possibly—an Original Literature.

Mr. Paulding is understood to be still in working

order ; as his recent romance, and pungent political letter abundantly prove. Although he is not given to long speeches, he can yet guide a thumb and forefinger to level his anti-Post letters at the 'woolly-headed fanatics' of whatever complexion: and, perhaps, in virtue of this last avowal on his part, hints have been bruited, that the hand which furbished up the papers of the Salmagundi may not have been ignorant of the management of these Studies of the town. The hints, however, as I understand, have confused other and younger members of the author's family in the charge ;—on what ground, or with what semblance of truth, it would hardly become me, who am ignorant of the parties, to judge. I trust though, that if the gentlemen alluded to are addicted to pen-work, they will do no discredit to the elder of the name ; and if they should break ground with no worse laid furrow than the pages of the LORGNETTE, I hope they may reap praise enough to pay them for their pains.

Several young gentlemen just having completed their studies, or recently returned from abroad, are upon my publisher's list of reported authors. I would gladly do them any reasonable favor. But upon my conscience, it will cost too dearly to say *peccavi* or *peccabo*, to any of the platulencies of boyhood. Errors of manner and thought are become ingrained ; these are not the wanton fancies of a fresh-read youth, however promising his wit ; and though these young gentlemen do not deny the imputation for themselves, I must, in self-defence, abjure the charge, and settle into the repose of that maturity, which years only can give.

There are still others, the list now running to thirty, who in their peculiar circles, are the undoubted Timons. Of some of these, whose names are at command, I can find no trace either in the literary or moral world ; and if so be they have ever used a pen, I suspect they must belong to that numerous, and deserving class, who are immortalized by contribution of thrilling tales to weekly newspapers, and whose readers are devout admirers of Prof. Ingraham, and extravagantly fond of peanuts.

I have been not a little amused and chagrined, my dear Fritz, on hearing these letters attributed to an eminent beau of the town—a man well posted indeed, in all social chat, and lively enough as the times go ; but for the matter of this new charge, I must beg to enter a modest caveat in his behalf. John Timon is no professional beau, and whatever the short-comings of his mental or moral endowments, they have had none of that social rasping of the town, which cuts away the native qualities, and leaves a be-padded, and be-curled woman of a man. The study of mirror and cosmetics has never engrossed him to the neglect of dictionaries: and whatever else may be said in a hard way, let him not be condemned, as one who hangs his social ventures upon the heel of his pump, and who tunes his talk to the play of a moustache.

Nor is it supposable that a man, devoting four or five hours of the best of the day to the mirror, or to the practice of a polka, can have leisure or industry for this weekly labor. I have no faith in those literateurs who are forever boasting of the ease of writing;—as if a dozen pages for the perusal, and the thought of a thousand, could be thrown off in the interval between cigars. I have too much respect for the public, and for you, Fritz, to palm on your ear any such crude batter of words. Time and attention are due even to the humility of this toil; and though it does not smell of the lamp, or show such touches of the file as it ought to do, be assured that it is honored with the task-work of determined handling. I have very little respect for those reputations for quick parts, which are maintained by a boasted carelessness and rapidity of style: and if an unknown observer might hazard the remark, our authors and authorlings, the half of them at least, would do well to hammer at their metal far more vigorously, and with better directed strokes, if they hope to put such temper in it as will hold an edge, and cut.

Even now, Fritz, but half has been said, which might be said upon the authors of the town: a host remains, even omitting the entire company of our deserving and attractive authoresses. An apology, perhaps, is due for having alluded more particularly to such as have become associated by careless suspicion with our correspondence; should the correspondence continue, Fritz, not a pen-man, or a *claqueur*, but shall be honored.

In alluding to individuals by name, in the present paper, I have confined myself strictly to such as have rendered the publicity warrantable by their writings; and in alluding to their mental habit and disposition, I have scrupulously forborne to meddle with the interior social life, where it appears to me no gentleman can safely venture with his pen.

Much might be said, however, of the social position of authors; and the influence of literary cultivation upon the graduation of the fashionable scale of the town; the topic must lie over to some season when the game is a little more plump; and then, 'please Providence,' I will throw a yellow cartridge into the whole flock of poets and poetasters.

My publisher informs me, as the sheets are passing through the press, that the twelve numbers now issued will make a fair-sized volume; you may possibly, therefore, my dear Fritz, miss the ensuing week your accustomed visitant: and whether it will make its appearance the coming month, will depend very much on my own whim, and the humor of the town. But do not be misled, Fritz;—it has been thrown out by some that the LORGNETTE was nothing more than an eccentric charity; and one very grave and important publisher assured me that it was wholly paid for by its author, and then placed, printed and bound, in the hands of the publisher. The dear public will allow me to correct this error, and to assure them that though they may laugh at my labor, they are paying for the laugh.

Nor is this said in vanity, but in justification; for nothing seems to me a more absurd charity than for a man to publish his thoughts, when the public do not care enough for his thought, to pay for the printing. Such a man (and on this point my opinion will be obnoxious to many town-authors) had much better every way drop his surplus pence into the parish poor box: in that case, he may console himself with knowing that no one is pestered with his thought, and that some poor souls may possibly be stuffing their bellies with his money.

John Timon neither owes any man, nor is he any man's creditor. He leaves off, if he leaves off, as fairly as he started; and he will be at liberty to begin, whenever his whim directs.

Not a tithe of the material is yet exhausted; the whole race of belles are still sighing for their portraits; the salon is without its picture; even the politicians and the churches have been sadly neglected. A chapter might easily be based upon the vigorous researches, the family garrulity, and the monthly chocolate of our New York Historical Society. The journals, from the heavy counting-room leviathan, to the motley, home-spun, patch-quilt of the Tribune, are topics full of fatness; and even the editor of the Democratic might find, that though modesty and dignity may forbid me to follow him to his social haunts, that I can unravel some of his slave-knotted yarns, and put a finger to his moral pulse, that will explain much of his political weakness.

And now a word to those who cannot determine 'what the deuce I would be at,' and who are bothered by the sharp moral hits, that are scattered over my social paintings. They neither see the point, or the meaning of such things; they are deserving of sympathy. You will remember our quondam Yankee friend, fresh from country cookery, who could make nothing, in the Parisian restaurant, of a *filet au sauce piquante*—who would have liked the beef indeed tolerably well, if they had not spilled the cruet upon it!

The Grecians, on a time, used to go to their Bacchan festivities with spears muffled in garlands—showing the grace of flowers, but always ready to prick a foe. Fritz,—the town-life is my Bacchan festival; the town-topics are my Bacchan sport; and this pen is my Bacchan *thyrsus!*

TIMON.

www.ingramcontent.com/pod-product-compliance
Lightning Source LLC
LaVergne TN
LVHW020243110826
845151LV00003B/1019

* 9 7 8 1 4 2 5 5 3 0 9 5 2 *